Gary Greenwald has provided vital insight for every Christian who desires to be whole in the Spirit of God without being controlled by other spirits. The truths found in **SEDUCTIONS EXPOSED** will make Christians free and fortify them against the attack of unscriptural influences.

— Dr. Bill Hamon

After reading **SEDUCTIONS EXPOSED**, I can wholeheartedly recommend it as being sound in doctrine and prophetic insight into the kingdom of darkness and wickedness. Pastor Gary thoroughly covers the subject of demonic influences and exposes and unmasks satanic infiltration, not only in the secular world, but also in the religious world. This book *must* be in the hands of every believer!

— Dr. Emanuele Cannistraci

Published in Santa Ana, California, by Eagle's Nest Publications, a division of Eagle's Nest Christian Fellowship.

First Printing, April 1989

Cover photo by Dressler Studios, Tustin, California.

ISBN   0-929748-00-X
Library of Congress Number: 88-82484

Printed in the United States of America.

SEDUCTIONS
· E X P O S E D ·
The Spiritual Dynamics of Relationships

By Gary L. Greenwald

Eagle's Nest Publications
Santa Ana, CA

About the author –

Gary Greenwald became a Christian as a young boy but it was not until the dynamic infilling of the Holy Spirit at age 26 that his life became a powerfully effective witness for the Lord. After several years of teaching Bible studies, showing Christian movies to young people, and supporting various outreach ministries, God used Gary to launch the Eagle's Nest Christian Fellowship on what he called the "Five W's" of ministry: the WORSHIP, the WORD, the WITNESS, the WORKS, and the WARFARE.

Pastor Gary has traveled throughout the United States and many other countries, preaching and ministering with signs following. Having been miraculously healed and delivered from polio, encephalitis, illeitis, and Bright's disease, God has anointed him with special gifts of healings, faith, and miracles.

Pastor Gary's popular television program, "Eagle's Food from the Eagle's Nest" has been seen across America. Speaking on contemporary subjects as well as sound Biblical theology, his unique messages have brought salvation, healing, and deliverance to multitudes.

Many have characterized Pastor Gary as a man after God's own heart. His vision includes raising up the Eagle's Nest as an evangelistic center and equipping the end-time army of the Lord. Because of his wide-ranging accomplishments, he has been recently honored with an honorary doctorate from Christian International School of Theology.

To all God's wounded soldiers who have fallen on the spiritual battlefield, I dedicate this book in hopes that multitudes will be restored to full service and others will perceive satan's seductions long before they bring injury.

My deepest thank you to my faithful staff for their support, my father and mother for their laborious proofreading, Dr. Bill Hamon for his scholarly critiquing, and especially Inga Peterson, my publications director, who spent long, painstaking hours researching my messages and compiling the threads of revelation that tie these chapters together.

Without the grace of my Lord and Saviour, Jesus Christ and the inspiring breath of God's Holy Spirit, these pages would never have come to life.

— Gary L. Greenwald

FOREWORD

A spiritual battle is raging all around us. Without discernment into the spiritual realm, the church will never grow to her position of conquering authority and maturity. Because of the operation of evil spirits, human spirits, and the Spirit of the Lord, and a lack of discernment as to which is operating in different situations, confusion seems to abound in individuals, in churches and in pulpits around the world. Many leaders are blowing trumpets that are giving uncertain sounds regarding the work of differing spirits because they do not understand the spiritual battle themselves.

In this book, **Seductions Exposed,** Pastor Gary Greenwald skillfully examines and exposes the manipulating spiritual activity that surrounds every Christian on a daily basis. Today, as never before, Christians are opening their eyes and becoming aware of the maneuvers, manipulations, and deceptions that are occurring in the spirit world.

This book offers answers and keys. Jesus Himself said, "And you shall know the truth and the truth shall set you free."

> — Pastor Rick Godwin
> Eagle's Nest Christian Fellowship
> San Antonio, Texas

Contents

SEDUCTIONS EXPOSED

THE SPIRITUAL DYNAMICS OF RELATIONSHIPS

CONTENTS

Introduction

S

JU   **;!!!**

Fasten y...   ...re going to take
you on a rolle   ...so many beautiful
Christians are   ...elationships, weird
manipulations at   ...s, and a succession of
unexplainable curs...

Listen to this hori... ...estimony by a sweet, God-fearing young woman ...io received God's wisdom, understanding, and deliverance from the messages in this book. She begins... "I recently discovered that in my toddler years an aunt, who was also a high priestess in a satanic church, had placed a curse upon me. As a child I was always sickly, unhappy, and lonely. I was constantly rejected, belittled, and intimidated by the other children. My only friends were children, who for one reason or another, were also considered outcasts. Associating with those children only reinforced my feelings of rejection and low self-esteem.

"My home life was also unhappy. No matter how hard I tried, I never seemed able to please my mother or live up to her standards of perfection. She spared no words in telling me so. By the time I was in my mid-teens, I was looking for a way out of the house. One night I went to a party with my boyfriend, drank too much alcohol, and actually passed out in the front seat of his car. He raped me. Being totally devastated, I broke up with him because I had wanted to remain a virgin for the man I married. But even though I felt dirty and ruined, I was strangely drawn back to him.... Later I learned I had developed a soul tie to him through our sexual involvement. I did not love him, but thought that since my life was ruined and my dreams were shattered, I might as well take this opportunity to leave home so I married him.

"As my husband he was basically a good person, but he had a violent temper and would often abuse me physically. Because he also suffered from oppression and rejection, he would belittle and falsely accuse me constantly. Eventually, he also began sleeping with other women on a regular basis. After five unhappy years, we were divorced. But like so many others, I went from one unhappy marriage into another that was also doomed to fail. My second husband was unfaithful as well.

"Scared and hurting, with the responsibility of three small children to raise alone, I cried out to God for help and accepted Jesus Christ as my saviour. I found a little church where the pastor had a desire for the things of God, and I grew in the knowledge and understanding of God's ways. After experiencing God's blessings for a while, some men came into that body of believers and introduced the 'shepherding' doctrine of 'absolute submission' to the leadership. Gradually, a wrong spirit came upon that church. During that time there was a young man in the church who decided I was to be his wife. Even though I felt no attraction to him, he enlisted the help of the church

Introduction

leadership and pressured me into a marriage. I later learned this was a form of charismatic witchcraft and manipulation.

"How did all this happen? The leaders and other people in the church were constantly telling me that I was blessed with a rare opportunity to marry a fine Christian husband. Hearing so many voices, I became confused and began to doubt my own feelings and my own ability to make decisions, or even to hear God's voice. The young man seemed very spiritual and would often quote scriptures to me. He ultimately used a maneuver on me that I could not resist. He won the heart of my son who wanted a father more than anything in the world. Through the pressure and manipulation of the leaders, the young man, and my son, I finally consented to marry him. However, after we were married I had no desire for him and found myself unable to enter into a physical relationship with him. He literally raped me on our wedding night. Then I became deathly sick.... People thought I had cancer because my flesh was withering away. Through some godly counsel I was able to break away from this man, annul the marriage, and regain my health. But not before my son had become estranged from me. The young man had convinced my son that I had become possessed of the devil and that was why I had rejected him! That same young man later remarried but shortly thereafter left his new wife for another man. He had also been the prey of satanic deception, manipulation, and sexual seduction.

"Eventually, the Lord led me to Pastor Gary's messages, and the Holy Spirit used them to reveal that the source of my continual problems was the curse my aunt had placed on my life. I have broken free of the charismatic witchcraft and the manipulation that came from my so-called "Christian" husband, and I have broken the soul ties from my previous marriages as I have received knowledge in those areas. Because of ignorance, my children all suffered from the same rejection, abuse, and manipulation that I did. With God's help they also have been healed and restored and now serve the Lord. My relationship with my son is now completely restored, and he is a father raising his own children with godly wisdom."

Just as the story of this young woman illustrates, many Christians have been deceived and their lives destroyed because they have not understood basic principles of the Word of God. When I realized that Jesus had given us the keys of the kingdom, I began a journey in the spirit to discover certain keys that would unlock the truths of why some Christians were cursed and their lives were torn apart. Many of these keys are contained in this book.

In the chapter on "The Dangerous Transference of Spirits," I share many of the aspects of how individuals are influenced by other individuals and the spirits (attitudes, beliefs, and morals) that characterize them. I discuss the influence of relationships, crowds, churches, anointed leaders, and the spirit of the world. Later in the book, I will scripturally show that we become like those with whom we associate. We take on their characteristics, their traits (whether good or evil), and even their anointings and mantles.

In the chapter on "Soul Ties," I examine the strong bonds that people form when they are in relationships, especially sexual ones, which cause their lives to be linked soulishly and physically. This powerful bonding explains why so many Christians still find themselves longing for previous partners.

In the chapter on "Charismatic Witchcraft," I take you on a discovery of how Christians misuse God's gifts, His prophetic mantle, and even how they misuse the authority that He has given them in the spiritual realm to manipulate and control others. This kind of spiritual seduction has brought the destruction of many lives in our churches.

Finally, in the chapter on "Abominable Occultic Objects and Practices," I uncover in the Word how anyone who brings an accursed object into his home or wears it on his body actually invites curses and evil spirits to oppress his life. I share how certain rather common occultic practices are forbidden by God and open doors of spiritual and physical oppression.

As we examine these keys of the kingdom, I believe your eyes will be opened as mine were, and many of the truths of the Bible will splash upon your understanding as God gives you a revelation of why many Christians often cannot live in victory. It is my prayer that after reading these chapters, you will become extremely cautious about those with whom you associate, you will keep your body sanctified in honor unto the Lord, you will never manipulate others with your gifts or prayers, and you will avoid wearing certain jewelry and bringing certain objects into your home as well as avoiding practices that God considers occultic and abominable. Unfortunately, many of these forbidden practices have already sneaked into the church and seduced many away from the true doctrines of Christ.

If you find your own life snared in one of the areas discussed here, this is the time to judge yourself and repent before God's judgment comes into your life. Hebrews tells us that every sin receives a just recompense of reward, and you cannot indulge yourself in forbidden practices and relationships and the misuse of God's gifts without the Holy Spirit being close behind "to chasten those whom He loves...."

THE DANGEROUS TRANSFERENCE OF SPIRITS

Seducing Attitudes

Have you ever wondered why you are more comfortable with some people than with others? Have you considered that perhaps you might be subconsciously seeking out friends, business associates, or even churches with the same spirit and attitudes that you have? According to Webster's dictionary, one of the definitions of the word "spirit" is the "prevailing attitude or characteristics of something or someone."

Every mother instinctively knows about the transference of spirits. She knows that when little Johnny plays with the rebellious, disobedient little boy next door, Johnny may come home with a rebellious, disobedient attitude or spirit that she has to discipline out of him. She knows which children in the neighborhood influence her child for good and which ones have a negative influence. By association, they may take on the same attitudes and actions. Paul warns in I Corinthians 15:33 [AMP],

SEDUCTIONS EXPOSED

*"Do not be so deceived and misled! Evil **companionships, (communion, associations)** corrupt and deprave good manners and morals and character."*

Did you know that you cannot be anywhere in this world without being influenced to some degree by the spirits around you? You may walk into a nightclub, thinking it will have no effect on you because you are a child of God. You may even plan to go into that nightclub with its loud, sensual music, heavy drinking, illicit drug trafficking, and sexual interplay thinking you can evangelize that place for Jesus Christ. But there is another spirit at work in that atmosphere. It is the spirit of satan and this world system, and it will affect your attitudes and may even transfer to you if you are exposed to it for very long.

Why is it that a young person may become involved in hard rock music, go to rock concerts, and be introduced to the world of sex, drugs, and loud rock music, and then suddenly be changed overnight to become like another person? He may lose interest in school, and he may drastically change his appearance and even the type of clothes he wears. He may become rebellious and not want to obey or even listen to his parents anymore. How can this radical change be explained unless there is a transference from the rock stars and their followers to that person?

Why is it that a young, virginal girl may go to work for a business firm and within six months she has been seduced by one of the partners? Could it be that a spirit of carnality and promiscuity has been transferred to her by the playboy businessmen in her office? Or, why is it that a godly young man or woman may go away to college and come home one day and deny that he even believes in God anymore? Could the prevailing spirits of intellectualism and philosophy have gradually transferred to him and destroyed his belief in God?

On the other hand, why is it a worldly and ungodly person may come into a church service, where there is a mighty anointing on the praise and worship and a convicting power on the message, and that person is compelled to run to the altar and accept Jesus into his life? Why is it, unless the Spirit of God is strongly influencing that person, convicting him of sin and drawing him into the family of God? Wherever there is a strong spirit present, it can influence and eventually transfer to you. Proverbs 13:20 says it this way,

> *"He that walketh with wise men shall be wise: but a companion of fools shall be destroyed."*

Only by walking in the Spirit of God can a person be protected from the transfer of powerful, negative spirits because according to I John 4:4, *"...greater is He that is in you, than he that is in the world."*

I want to share with you about the dangerous transference of spirits because it is responsible for the breakup of families, it has alienated multitudes of close friends and relatives from one another, it has torn numerous churches apart, and it has caused many marriages to disintegrate. It grieves me that I have seen this dangerous transference operating in so many churches of Jesus Christ. Someone will come into a church with a different spirit or a wrong spirit, and it may cause division and strife and actually split that church.

You may find it difficult to accept the concept of a transference of spirits because you do not feel that those around you can have such a powerful effect on you. Controversial subjects like this one are often rejected before they are fully tested. This is not only true in spiritual concepts, but also in the scientific realm. Galileo experienced rejection, ridicule, and even excommunication from the Roman Catholic church for daring to publish his findings that the world was round and not flat as everyone in his day had previously believed. People of that day thought their theology demanded a flat earth – they thought if they accepted the idea of a round earth, the truth of their religious beliefs would be threatened. It was not until after his death that Galileo's scientific achievements were recognized and accepted as truth, and even shown to be verified by the Bible.

We will examine attitudes and characteristics of people, the spiritual influence of worldliness and evil spirits, and the good transference of mantles and anointings from other people of God. I want you to prayerfully consider what I have to say about the transference of spirits. Ask the Holy Spirit to give you His wisdom and understanding because this vital subject can only be spiritually understood. I Corinthians 2:12-14 says,

"Now we have received, not the spirit of the world, but the Spirit which is of God; that we might know the things that are freely given to us of God. Which things also we speak, not in the words which man's wisdom teacheth, but which the

The Dangerous Transference of Spirits

Holy Ghost teacheth; comparing spiritual things with spiritual. But the natural (worldly) man receiveth not the things of the Spirit of God: for they are foolishness unto him: neither can he know them, because they are spiritually discerned."

Only by becoming aware of the powerful effect that other individuals, groups, and the media often exert on you, can you protect yourself and others from negative and destructive influences and transferences.

To begin with, successful relationships can only be maintained when individuals have a unity of spirit. If someone with a negative or even different spirit associates with an individual or joins his group, all unity and harmony may eventually be disrupted. Families, friendships, marriages, and churches have to maintain a kindred (or similar) spirit. They must have a similar vision if they are to accomplish their goals and live in harmonious unity. God asks us in Amos 3:3,

"Can two walk together, except they be agreed?"

In essence, God is asking if two people can have harmony in their relationship or Christian fellowship if they have a different spirit – He is speaking of things such as attitudes, beliefs, vision, morality, and ethics.

Ruler Spirits

This phenomenon of transference occurs everywhere. There are even ruler spirits over cities and countries that affect and characterize the people that live in those cities and countries. For example, there is a gambling and party spirit over the city of Las Vegas. It becomes difficult for anyone to go there and stay for any length of time without finding himself influenced by that same party spirit. There are spirits of self-promotion, false glamour, and sexual promiscuity over the city of Hollywood. People who go there often become seduced by those same spirits. On the other hand, whenever I visit Hawaii, I battle the influence of a spirit of dropout laziness that characterizes the "hang-loose" attitude of the islands. There are also spirits that characterize the people of certain nations and cities. Germans are reputed to be industrious, clean people, while Italians have a freedom of expression and a zest for life that characterizes them as hopeless romantics.

Because it is just as easy to acquire negative characteristics as positive ones, the only way to avoid the transfer of negative spirits is to stay in the Word of God daily, to walk in the Spirit of God, and to use the spiritual armor God has given us through Jesus Christ. Paul reminds us of what we are up against in Ephesians 6:11-12, when he says,

> *"Put on the whole armor of God, that ye may be able to stand against the wiles (or schemes) of the devil. For we wrestle not against flesh and blood, but against principalities, against powers, against the rulers of the darkness of this world, against spiritual wickedness in high places."*

I counseled and discipled a young man several years ago whom I had brought to the Lord. Since I worked as a salesman at the time, I spent a great deal of time with him, even taking him with me in my car while I drove from customer to customer. I taught him many valuable truths about the Lord and the Bible and shared with him how to walk strongly with the Lord. One day he informed me that he was moving to San Francisco. Although I did not feel he was strong and mature enough in the Lord to withstand the spirit of that city, he insisted on going. I warned him to stay in the Word of God daily, to fellowship with other Christians, and to find a strong church immediately. He told me not to worry, that he had been in San Francisco before, and the spirit of the city had not affected him. To my chagrin, I found out later that he had backslidden and become a homosexual. There had been a transference of the spirit of homosexuality to him. This is not to say that everyone who goes to San Francisco will become gay but the well-known concentration of homosexuals there is evidence of the prevailing spirit at work.

In the Old Testament, God destroyed the cities of Sodom and Gomorrah because the ruler spirits of homosexuality, perversion, and greed had spread like malignant cancer to all the people of those cities so that not even ten righteous people could be found living there. In intercession, Abraham begged God not to destroy the people of those cities. In Genesis 18:32 [AMP], Abraham pleaded with God,

> *"...Oh, let not the Lord be angry, and I will speak again only this once. Suppose ten [righteous people] shall be found there. And [the Lord] said, I will not destroy it for ten's sake."*

Sadly though, there were not even ten righteous people living there who had not been corrupted by the spirits ruling over those cities.

As a young Christian, I often questioned why the children of Israel were commanded by God to utterly destroy all the nations occupying the promised land. God even told them to destroy the infants and animals and not to take any of their possessions into their households. In my poor understanding of scripture at the time, God seemed cruel and unloving. But as the Lord has revealed to me an understanding of the powerful and dangerous transference of spirits, I now know it was God's justice and kindness to issue such a strong decree. In His sovereignty, God knew that those ungodly nations would not repent. God also knew the children of Israel would become polluted by their sins and idolatries – He knew evil spirits would transfer to His people. Deuteronomy 20:16-18 [AMP] explains,

> *"But of the cities of these people, which the Lord your God gives you for an inheritance, you shall save alive nothing that breathes. But you shall utterly exterminate them, the Hittites, the Amorites, the Canaanites, the Perizzites, the Hivites, and the Jebusites; as the Lord your God has commanded you; so they may not teach you all the abominable practices they have carried on for their gods, and so cause you to sin against the Lord your God."*

In other words, by association they would teach their abominable practices to God's children. In recent times, archeologists have uncovered evidence that those nations were indeed extremely morally corrupt, even sacrificing their own children to their gods of wood and stone.

Evil Associations

I know of a lovely Christian girl whose father is the pastor of a large, successful charismatic church. She has been raised in a godly home where Jesus is exalted. Even though she professed Jesus as her saviour as a young girl, as she grew into a young woman she found excitement in the party scene, in drinking, and associating with worldly men. However, whenever she was around her church and Christian friends, she repented, read her Bible, and lived godly. Today she is besieged by turmoil. Sometimes she succumbs to satan's pounding temptations and the lure of her worldly friends. When she is around the nightclubs and parties, this godly Christian girl takes on another spirit entirely.... She becomes carnal and sensuous. She is faced with an awesome choice – the pleasures of sin for a season or a godly life in Christ for eternity.

A person or group with strong spiritual traits can actually transfer those traits by association to another person or group. In the previous case of the young pastor's daughter, there was a transference of this world's spirit to her. As I began this chapter, Paul strongly warns us in I Corinthians 15:33-34 [AMP],

> *"Do not be so deceived and misled! Evil **companion-ships, (communion, associations**) corrupt and deprave good manners and morals and character. Awake (from your drunken stupor and return) to sober sense and your right minds, and sin no more. For some of you have not the*

knowledge of God – you are utterly and wilfully and disgracefully ignorant, and continue to be so, lacking the sense of God's presence and all true knowledge of Him. I say this to your shame."

You *will* become like your friends and associates!

Because it seems to be far easier for compromising Christians to be influenced by the wrong in others than to influence them for good, Paul adamantly warns us not to date or marry unbelievers and not to associate closely with people of the world. II Corinthians 6:14-18 warns,

> *"Be ye **not** unequally yoked together with unbelievers: for what fellowship hath righteousness with unrighteousness? and what communion hath light with darkness?.. or what part hath he that believeth with an infidel?.. for ye are the temple of the living God: as God hath said, I will dwell in them, and walk in them; and I will be their God, and they shall be My people. Wherefore come out and be ye separate, saith the Lord, and touch not the unclean thing; and I will receive you, and I will be a Father unto you..."*

It can even become spiritually hazardous to associate too closely with other Christians who do not have the same desires, visions, and attitudes that you have because their different spirits – desires, visions, and attitudes – may transfer to you. God's purpose and plan for your life may be thwarted if you allow others to manipulate and influence you.

To illustrate how a person can lose out with God, I remember the pathetic and quite horrendous story of a sweet, young Christian girl who was one of the most dedicated intercessors of the church I attended some years ago. She was constantly studying her Bible, going to church every service, and God used her mightily to counsel and minister to others. She was believing God for a Christian mate – a godly man who loved Jesus and put Him first in his life. One day a backslidden Christian young man came into her life. His god was tennis and partying, although at one time he had taught home Bible studies. When he began dating this young lady, he started going back to church and gave a very convincing performance as a committed and repentant young man. He quoted scriptures and attended Bible studies with her. For all appearances, he had come back to the Lord under the influence of this young lady's life.

Some of those who had known about the young man's past worldliness warned this young lady to take her time to really get to know him for they were not fully convinced that he had changed. But, like most young people in love, she felt that she could throw caution to the wind. After a short courtship, they announced their engagement and were soon married. The grievous part of this story is that after the honeymoon, the young man decided he no longer wished to be married. Furthermore, he wanted nothing to do with God. He immediately called up old girlfriends and got back into the tennis scene, and he never again went to church as long as they were married.

For a couple of years, this girl tried to maintain a walk with the Lord, but the influence of her husband and the discouragement of a bad marriage slowly drew her away from the church. Before long, she had little place in her life for God. I was amazed as I watched her become more and more worldly. She found a position working for the airlines and began dating numerous pilots. She left her old Christian friends behind for a fast, new group of associations. In the end, this young lady, who was mightily used of God with gifts and anointing so obvious to everyone, lost out with God. Because of an association with a worldly and carnal young man, she slowly became worldly and carnal herself, and she abandoned her strong walk with the Lord.

Birds of a Feather Flock Together

You have heard the expression, "birds of a feather flock together." As a minister, I have observed over and over that where you find an individual with strange behavior, unproven and unorthodox doctrines, or rebellion in his heart, those in his cluster of associations may often have the same characteristics. The other pastors on my staff and I continually watch for potential trouble makers by keeping an eye on different clusters in the church.

For example, we had to deal with a young lady who was manipulating and dominating in nature. She tried to control people in her Bible study, she had strange doctrines, she claimed to be a prophetess of God, and she enjoyed having people doing her will. We noticed several other young girls who began to associate with her in the church. All of them started making strange hand motions during the services. They would walk like single-file clones, imitating their leader and sometimes even running into people during the intercessory prayer meetings. If the leader laid down on the floor, the others would do the same. Her influence and control over them became so strong that they would not sit down in the pew during the church service until she nodded and gave her approval. When we attempted to redeem her, she refused the counsel and discipline of the leadership. Finally, because her influence began to spread to more and more people, we had to ask her to leave the church. Sadly, even after she and her friends left the church, many who attended her Bible study, including some of the usher staff and a number of the intercessors, also left the church. They had embraced some of the same strange doctrines and rebellious attitudes that characterized her!

Even great and wise men will become like those with whom they surround themselves. King Solomon was wiser and had more understanding than any other man who ever lived, and yet because he disobeyed God's command and married heathen wives, he eventually partook of their sins and sacrificed to their strange gods. With all his wisdom, he still became deceived and could not withstand the influence of his wives. I Kings 1:1-3 explains,

> *"But King Solomon loved many strange women, together with the daughter of Pharaoh, women of the Moabites, Ammonites, Edomites, Zidonians and Hittites: of the nations concerning which the Lord said unto the children of Israel, ye shall not go in to them, neither shall they come in to you: for surely they will turn away your heart after their gods: Solomon clave unto these in love. And he had seven hundred wives, princesses, and three hundred concubines and his wives turned away his heart."*

Manipulating Intercessors

It has been my observation that intercessors often have a tendency to share their revelations with one another when they get together and before long find themselves agreeing with one another. Some time ago, a group of intercessors in my church exhibited this truth in a damaging way. The Eagle's Nest had gone through some strife and many of the people along with a large portion of the pastoral staff had left the church. One of the intercessors had received a revelation that God's judgment was about to fall upon me because of my supposed disobedience in leading the church a certain direction. After sharing her views with a few others, they all agreed that if I did not repent, I would be judged like King Nebuchadnezzar, who grew hair like an animal and ate grass in the field.

Because those intercessors had stepped out of their calling as supporters and prayer warriors, they had been deceived into believing they had more vision for the church than their pastor. Their pride had opened them up to a spirit of error. The role of intercessors is to birth the vision received by the leadership through prayer, not to discuss what they may see in the spiritual realm with others. Those intercessors were trying to manipulate me with their warnings and in doing so had fallen into fleshly manipulation. When they confronted me, I exhorted them, telling them they had stepped out of their calling. One strong intercessor had led them into their deception. Most of them left the church over the incident and some of them have since then gone through grievous marital problems, divorces, and financial shortages.

On the other hand, intercessors who are in one accord and have truly submitted themselves to the will of God can have a powerful godly influence on individuals, churches, and even nations. For example, some of the intercessors of the Eagle's Nest decided they would put their faith in action and close down a pornography store in Santa Ana. As they parked their van in front of the store and began to pray and to take authority over the powers of darkness ruling over the store, the van suddenly began to shake with God's presence. They felt inspired to drive around the block seven times as they continued to pray and praise God for the victory. As they turned the corner the seventh time, they could not even get near the building because of all the police cars that were in the process of raiding the store and closing its doors!

Close Encounters of the Worst Kind

Because we take on the attitudes of those around us, there are times in our lives when God allows and even ordains separations from family, friends, and even leaders over us. He does not want their negative attitudes and character flaws to be transferred to us by association. For instance, David was driven from King Saul's court so he would not pick up Saul's disobedient, rebellious, and evil spirit. I believe, in His sovereignty, God saw if he allowed David to stay in Saul's court, he might become like Saul. In the wilderness where God could deal with David on a one to one basis, David became a man after God's own heart. He became like God because he spent time with God!

SEDUCTIONS EXPOSED

There are hundreds of horror stories of multitudes being corrupted by evil leaders. One very extreme, but undeniable example of a leader's evil spirit transferring to and transforming an entire nation is that of Adolph Hitler[1]. Taking advantage of the economic chaos that existed in post-World War I Germany, Hitler used clever, emotional rhetoric to draw the people to his leadership and at the same time to stir up hatred toward the Jews. By falsely convincing the German people of their racial superiority, Hitler focused the blame for the economic depression upon the Jews. His hatred, anger, and violent terror spread to the entire German hierarchy and they willingly helped him exterminate millions of Jews.

As we have pointed out, we often see the transference of spirits working in a negative way through associations. When Moses was giving the Israelites instructions for war and conquering the promised land, he warned them not to allow any soldiers in the ranks who were fearful because that fear might spread to the entire army and cause their defeat. Deuteronomy 20:8 says,

> *"And the officers shall speak further unto the people, and they shall say, what man is fearful and faint-hearted? Let him go and return unto his house, lest his brother's heart faint as well as his heart."*

God did not want fear transferred from one man to another.

Crowd Effects

As you have seen, this transference of spirits (attitudes, ethics, morals, characteristics, etc.) takes place, not only between individuals, but also among large groups of people. I learned a hard, but valuable lesson in this area several years ago when I had a crusade exposing the evils of satanic rock music in Dallas, Texas. Because we wanted to reach the unsaved young people heavily involved in hard rock music, we advertised the crusade only on secular radio stations that played rock music. Unfortunately, we neglected to inform the Christians, except for a small number working with us, of the crusade. As a result, the audience was predominately unsaved, hostile young people, many of whom openly worshipped hard rock music and its god, satan. Their very purpose in attending the meetings was to taunt me and disrupt the service. It was very difficult for me to preach in that oppressive atmosphere because the prevailing spirit was antichrist. Sadly, very few young people responded to Jesus Christ that night.

At our next crusade in Honolulu, Hawaii, we made certain that Christians from all over the island were informed of the meetings, and several thousand responded to support the meetings. Because Christians outnumbered the unsaved about two to one, the presence of the Lord was strongly sensed on the entire service. The praise and worship were exhilarating and set the tone for the entire evening. After I preached essentially the same message I had preached in Dallas, over five hundred young people gave their lives to Jesus – the spirit of Christ in the Christians overpowered the spirit of the world in the unsaved and allowed the Holy Spirit free access to their hearts.

On the other hand, whole groups of normally law abiding citizens can be transformed almost instantly to a destructive, hostile crowd when the spirit of a riot begins to control them. During the blackout in New York City several years ago, store windows were smashed and stores were broken into by people who normally would not even consider stealing. A spirit of riot and lawlessness had overtaken them. Paul tells us that the spirit of lawlessness is already present in the world, but will be even more evident in the future. According to II Thessalonians 2:7 [AMP],

> "For the mystery of lawlessness – that hidden principle of rebellion against constituted authority – is already at work in the world, [but it is] restrained only until he who restrains is taken out of the way."

Only by actively staying filled with the Spirit of God can a person withstand the powerful attacks unleashed by the forces of darkness in the end-times in which we live!

The Spirit of the World

The seducing powers of darkness are constantly trying to open us up to the spirit of the world. Do you ever find the inconsistencies and failures of your Christian walk frustrating? Sometimes Christians feel like the oil of the Holy Spirit has leaked out of them. They find themselves crying out with the Apostle Paul in Romans 7:19,24,

woul
delive

The mo
promises to
we break the
we so fickle ι

Our struggl
God or our self,
a human spirit w   ...t of
God or the spirit   ..ge, the spirit
of man may absoı   ...ıι it is in association
and fellowship witl.   ...ınthians 2:11-12 speaks of the
interaction of these three spirits.

> *"For what man knoweth the things of a man, save the **spirit**
> **of man** which is in him? even so the things of God knoweth
> no man, but the **Spirit of God**. Now we have received, not
> the **spirit of the world**, but the Spirit which is of God; that we
> might know the things that are freely given to us of God."*

Notice that Paul speaks of three distinct spirits: the
human spirit; the Spirit of God; and the spirit of the world.

Have you ever seen Christians who seem to want the
best of both worlds? They want to move in the power and
the authority of God, but they also want to partake of the
world – things like drinking, partying, and indulging in
fleshly desires. So what happens to Spirit-filled Christians who play with worldliness instead of forsaking it?

...ainst each other to in-
...spirit. Galatians 5:17 says,

...he carnal forces in us which are in-
...pirit of the world) lusteth (wars) against the
...d), and the Spirit against the flesh: and these
...rary the one to the other: so that ye canno: d the
...gs that ye would."

The spirit of the world is warring against the Spirit of God and to whatever spirit a person yields, that spirit will dominate his human spirit. A Christian who yields to both spirits finds himself in the middle of a vicious spiritual war. Romans 6:13 and 16 warns us not to yield ourselves to sin but to God, and that to whomever we yield ourselves, we become servants or slaves.

I want to show you how dangerous it is to associate with carnal people who are under the influence of the world's spirit. They are living in the flesh and you can receive a transference of their spirit, like clothes picking up smoke in a room. Samson, one of the judges of the children of Israel, discovered this truth in a very costly way. Because of his great strength, Samson was a terror to the Philistines, the enemies of Israel. Yet, he broke the commandment of God not to marry a heathen woman when he took the woman of Timnath as his wife against the advice of his godly parents. Later he visited a harlot in Gaza and lay with her. When he found the beautiful Delilah, he fell in love (or lust) and fornicated with her. In Judges 16:15, the Philistines offered Delilah a fabulous sum of silver to seduce Samson into revealing the secret of his awesome strength. Samson had continually harassed and defeated them. When the Spirit of the Lord came upon him, he was able to do amazing things and no man could withstand him. For example, one day he killed a thousand Philistines with the jawbone of an ass.

Because Samson was able to withstand any physical enemy, he thought he could withstand the spiritual forces of the Philistines also. Delilah deliberately seduced Samson in his weak area in order to destroy him. At first, he was able to withstand her lies and seductions, but the spirit of the world in her gradually overcame him to the point that he did not realize that the Spirit of God had left him. When he finally told her the secret of his great strength was his uncut hair, she immediately lulled him to sleep and sent for a barber. Samson awoke from his stupor to find himself in the lap of the world. Sadly, Judges 16:20 [AMP] says of him,

> *"...and he awoke out of his sleep, and said, I will go out as I have time after time, and shake myself free. For Samson did not know the Lord had departed from him."*

Samson spent the rest of his life a blind slave of the Philistines (the world system). Only in his death, did God grant him vindication against his enemies. Like so many Christians, Samson thought he could play with the world and not have the spirit of the world destroy his strength in God.

Unfortunately, some Christian leaders fall into the deception that because of their "success" in ministry certain commandments in the Bible do not apply to them. Because God's blessing is on their lives in one area, they often assume God is blessing everything they do and somehow "bending" His laws for them. A traveling teacher and prophet, Al Houghton, recently shared with me how God had him confront such a leader. While pastoring a large church, the leader had divorced his wife and married one of his staff members. He felt his adultery and ultimate divorce was acceptable before God because he had a flourishing ministry with much exposure. Even so, the other leaders of his church were unable to condone his divorce and dismissed him. He subsequently began a new church across town.

Later, this pastor complained to Al that the people of his new church were extremely carnal and worldly. Most of them were divorced and living selfishly without any fear of God. The Lord gave Al the difficult task of telling this pastor that he was reaping what he had sowed. His people were living carnally because he had given them the example of a carnal, selfish life-style. His adultery was bringing forth fruit after its own kind in the lives of his flock. The counsel of the world had told this man that his divorce was justifiable and understandable, but in Psalm 1:1, God says,

> *"Blessed is the man who walketh not in the counsel of the ungodly..."*

Jesus affirmed, in Matthew 6:24, that,

> *"No man can serve two masters: for either he will hate the one, and love the other; or else he will hold to one, and despise the other. Ye cannot serve God and mammon (the spirit of the world system)."*

The Dangerous Transference of Spirits

If you are placing yourself in an atmosphere or relationship where you are receiving a transference of the spirit of this world, you are giving satan legal right to attack you, steal from you, afflict you, and possibly kill you. As a Christian, if you are dating an unbeliever, running around with carnal, worldly people, or contemplating marriage to one, you may be spiritually signing your own death warrant. Paul adamantly warns in Romans 8:6-7,

"For to be carnally minded is death; but to be spiritually minded is life and peace. Because the carnal mind is enmity (makes you the enemy) against God..."

During the past several years, I have watched how the beautiful daughter of some friends of mine has been seduced by the spirit of this world over and over because of wrong associations. As a teenager, she gave her life to the Lord and dedicated herself to serve Him with all her heart. She began to read her Bible and pray daily, and she attended church faithfully. But instead of forsaking her old worldly friends, she thought she could convert them to Jesus. While the motives of her heart were good and pure, she was not grounded and stable enough in the Lord and His ways to withstand the steady pull of the spirit of the world working through her friends. Soon she was back in the drinking and partying life-style.

Although the prayers and love of her family and the church kept her from completely turning her back on the Lord, she continued to play with the world. She began dating a young man who seemed very genuine in his feelings toward her but wanted nothing to do with Jesus.

At first she thought she could bring him to the Lord. But instead of her influencing him for good, he began drawing her into a more worldly life-style and his true nature became evident. He began to abuse her verbally and at times, physically. She would try to break free of the relationship and renew her vows to follow the Lord, but found herself strangely drawn back to that young man and the world time after time.

Eventually, things began to go wrong in her life. Her car began to break down very frequently, she was in several minor automobile accidents, and she became extremely prone to infections and often missed work. Yet she continued to live in a double manner – a Christian life-style at home and church and a carnal, worldly one with her friends. Her health continued to deteriorate to the point that she had to be hospitalized for a time with major surgery. Finally, she was in a serious accident and was arrested for drunk driving. Since then she has had to pay the consequences of her life of sin even though she has found forgiveness. This precious young girl has found that she cannot mix the things of the world with a holy life in Christ Jesus!

Hole in the Hedge

Many years ago, I knew a young man who was addicted to pornographic magazines and posters full of nude women. While he was a Christian, he had not yet been baptized in the Holy Spirit nor had he made Jesus the Lord of his life. As a Christian, he could not understand why he was driven by lust, wanting to possess every beautiful woman that crossed his path. When the Lord revealed to me that a spirit of lust had transferred to him through the pornographic magazines, I shared with him that the source of his problem was pornography. He repented and removed the magazines and posters from his home and office, destroying them. As he did so, the Lord set him free from that driving spirit of lust!

Movies, television, music, and magazines full of violence, pornography, lust, and immorality may transfer violence and lust to the person who fills his mind and time with such activities. Proverbs 4:23 warns,

> *"Keep thy heart (or protect your spirit) with all diligence; for out of it are the issues of life."*

Satan has masterfully enslaved millions of unregenerate human spirits and influenced many Christians with the spirit of this world through their eye and ear gates. Scripturally, satan has no legal right to afflict or oppress the believer who is under the covering of the shed blood of Jesus Christ. When a person indulges in sin and evil imaginations, God's divine blood hedge of protection may be broken, allowing evil spirits to oppress that person. Ecclesiastes 10:8 warns that,

> *"He who diggeth a pit shall fall into it; and he whoso breaketh a hedge, a serpent (demonic spirit) shall bite him."*

Paul understood that lust breaks down the hedge of protection and gives satan legal right to attack us when he wrote in Ephesians 4:22-23,27 [AMP],

SEDUCTIONS EXPOSED

*"Strip yourselves of your former nature – put off and discard your old unrenewed self – which characterized your previous manner of life and becomes corrupt through **lusts** and desires that spring from delusion; And be constantly renewed in the spirit of your mind – having a fresh mental and spiritual attitude;... Leave no [such] room or foothold for the devil – give no opportunity to him."*

Sin and disobedience will open a person to the transfer of ungodly spirits by "putting a hole in the hedge." There is a common deception among Christians, and even people of the world, who think that because they have reached a certain level of maturity or responsibility, they are immune from the effects of pornography, sensual movies, violent television programs, etc. Even though a Christian may be attending church, reading his Bible, and spending time in prayer, the spirit of the world is still able to seduce him if he gives place to it.

Several years ago, I asked the Lord if there was anything displeasing to Him in my life or in my home. He immediately pointed out the movie channels on the cable network I was subscribing to. Late at night, these movie channels showed R-rated and X-rated movies that I sometimes caught glimpses of while changing the channels. Even though I never watched those lustful and violent movies, the Lord impressed me not to even allow the appearance of evil by having these channels accessible to my television. The Lord prohibited me from giving opportunity for the spirit of the world to transfer to me in a moment of weakness. In another instance, I knew of a young man who suffered strong chest pains for months until he removed the cable stations that were stumbling him.

Because the spirit of the world is seducing in nature, a person can be slowly affected by it without even realizing that his attitudes have changed. Sexual immorality and profanity on television and in movies that once shocked and disturbed him, after a while do not seem "so bad." Like the frog that is placed in a pan of cold water which is slowly brought to boiling, he does not realize that he is being "cooked" until it is too late. Paul warns the believer in I Corinthians 10:12 [AMP],

> *"Therefore let any one who thinks he stands – who feels sure that he has a steadfast mind and is standing firm – take heed lest he fall [into sin]."*

No one, regardless of how strong his faith, his character, or his godly heritage is, can withstand the steady influence of the spirit of the world it he is not determined to submit to God and resist this world system.

Years ago a good friend and I would often go out on the streets, the beaches, and to the fairgrounds witnessing for Christ. We had devised a suitcase that actually contained a "PA" system that we carried as we preached in those public places. My friend had incredible boldness and a strong evangelistic anointing, but he also had a weakness – he liked beer and wine. We would go out to the restaurants together and order the finest wines as we sat over dinner. About that time, the Lord dealt with me that I was to give up wine. Whether wine was right or wrong was not the issue; I was not to be a stumbling block to the brethren. My friend continued to enjoy his wine and beer, however. Slowly, he began to drink more and more. Satan finally convinced him to go where the "real sinners" were – the nightclubs. Thinking he could witness while drinking and dancing, he was soon overcome by the spirit of the world. As his faith weakened, he fell back into the world.... He could not withstand the transference of the carnal spirit of this world in the nightclub atmosphere. The last time I saw my old friend, he was unclean, unshaven, sickly, and jobless. Satan had made a fool of that man who was once so zealous for God!

The Power of Suggestion

The news media continually carries reports that indicate the transference of spirits through the power of suggestive words and attitudes. Recently, the **Los Angeles Times** reported the case of the young boy who committed suicide after listening over and over to the song, "Suicide Solution" by the popular hard rock singer, Ozzie Osbourne. Obviously, he fell prey to a spirit of suicide. In another incident, the **Flint Journal** newspaper carried the following article on December 6, 1987.

> *"Without their parents' knowledge, a 13-year-old boy, his 10-year-old sister and two of their friends dialed a telephone service that offered recorded sexual messages. The recording, featuring a woman describing sexual acts in explicit language, apparently had a profound impact on the youngsters. The next day, the children's mother said the 10-year-old was molested by her two friends, and her 13-year-old brother had intercourse with another girl. The*

The Dangerous Transference of Spirits

incident, investigated by police and child protection agencies, has traumatized the lives of the families involved."

Sadly, these stories do not represent isolated incidents, but rather increasingly common occurrences. In each case, a very harmful spirit was transferred to the children. I believe parents are responsible for protecting the tender spirits of their children from the spirit of the world. Some children can be especially sensitive to what they see and hear as is vividly demonstrated by the following story. The headline in the **Weekly World News** of June 18, 1983, read "Teenage Dracula Bites 30 Children." According to the amazing article,

> *"Dozens of panic-stricken children shrieked in pain and terror as a real-life Dracula chased them down on the school ground and sank his teeth into their flesh. When the schoolyard horror ended, 30 youngsters, bleeding and hysterical, were rushed to a hospital where they were treated for shock, severe bite wounds and were given anti-infection inoculations. The nightmare attack was carried out by a 14-year-old student that police in Cleveland, England, would identify only as James. They said he went berserk shortly after he had watched a bloody Dracula movie on a local television station. He charged through the schoolyard during morning recess grabbing small children, holding them down and biting into their arms as they writhed in agony.' It was just like the movie, it was spooky,' said one of the boy's classmates, Angela Simmons, 13, 'He went wild and started attacking and biting the younger kids.'"*

Out of the thousands of young people who probably watched that same Dracula movie, why did James "go berserk?" I suspect that he was not raised in a Christian home, under the covering and protection of godly parents, and that he was particularly susceptible to a transference in the area of horror movies because of his particular heredity and personality. The Bible warns us that satan looks for opportunities to kill, steal from, and destroy us. I Peter 5:8 sternly cautions,

> *"Be sober, be vigilant; because your adversary the devil, as a roaring lion, walketh about, seeking whom he may devour."*

Heavenly and Hellish Heritage

Evil spirits are masters at attacking our weak areas. Not all children and adults are open and vulnerable to the spirit of the world and satan in the same areas, to the same degree, and at the same times in their lives. An experience that may be particularly devastating to one person may have little effect on another. One reason some people are more susceptible and sensitive to spiritual attack is their heritage. Exodus 20:5 speaks of ancestors that served other gods and worshipped graven images, exhorting,

> *"Thou shalt not bow down thyself to them, nor serve them: for I the Lord thy God am a jealous God, visiting the iniquity of the fathers upon the children unto the **third and fourth generation** of them that hate me."*

In other words, there is a transference of iniquity, or the tendency to sin in a particular area, down through the family line for several generations.

The Dangerous Transference of Spirits

Jeremiah echoes this same concept when he says, in Jeremiah 31:29,

> "...the fathers have eaten a sour grape, and the children's teeth are set on edge (the children suffer)."

Likewise, the children suffer because of the sins of their fathers. It is well known that children of alcoholics often become alcoholics; people who have suffered physical abuse as children have a very high incidence of becoming child abusers; and so continues the repetitious cycle in family after family... unless the curse is broken by the blood of Jesus, according to Galatians 3:13, and the person actively takes on the spiritual heritage of his Father in heaven.

On the other hand, a strong godly and spiritual inheritance serves to buttress and protect people from satanic attacks. Blessings like strength of character, finances, health, position, etc., are also passed from generation to generation. Deuteronomy 7:9 says,

> "Know therefore that the Lord thy God, He is God, the faithful God, which keepeth covenant and mercy with them that love Him and keep His commandments to a thousand generations..."

Speaking of the blessings and protection of his heritage, King David declares in Psalm 16:6,

> "The lines are fallen unto me in pleasant places; yea, I have a goodly heritage."

Spiritual covering from an authority figure like a father, husband, or church will also protect a person from the transfer of negative spirits. This is why the Bible emphasizes submission to authority and the necessity of belonging to a local body of believers. Hebrews 13:17 [AMP] says,

> *"Obey your spiritual leaders and submit to them – continually recognizing their authority over you; for they are constantly keeping watch over your souls and guarding your spiritual welfare, as men who will have to render an account [of their trust]..."*

Our counseling offices are filled with people who for one reason or another do not have proper spiritual covering.

A proper spiritual covering can protect a person from the transfer of the spirit of the world. For instance, one of my secretaries comes from a family of ten children, thirty grandchildren, and a growing number of great-grandchildren. The father is recognized and honored as both prophet and priest in the home by his children and the members of his community. Because both parents are strong Christians and pray for each person in the family daily, there is a strong spiritual covering over the entire family. Everyone in the family is saved and prosperous, and there is no divorce among all the children and grandchildren.

It grieves me when I see young men and women with godly parents and inheritance sell their birthright of Christian honor and protection, like Esau of old, for satan's bowl of worldly pottage....

Mantles and Anointings

There is an old axiom in the Christian world that says, "More is caught than taught." In other words, a person learns and is influenced more from the prevailing beliefs and attitudes of a person or group than by what is actually taught by that person or group. Just by being in association with someone or a group with a strong spirit, a person will be affected by those same prevailing attitudes. Because the Eagle's Nest strongly believes in the operation of the gifts of the Holy Spirit and the authority of the believer, the people raised up at the Eagle's Nest are also likely to emphasize their authority as believers and operating in the gifts of the Spirit. On the other hand, someone raised up in a church that excels in evangelism and missions outreach probably finds evangelism and mission work predominating in his life.

The Bible gives several illustrations of the transfer of mantles and anointings from associating with true men and women of God. Because Elisha determined to remain close to Elijah and serve him, he alone among the company of young prophets received the mantle of Elijah and the double portion of his anointing. Three times Elijah tested Elisha by asking him to remain behind as he went about doing the Lord's work, but Elisha refused to leave the side of his master. Elijah, knowing that he was about to be taken up to heaven, asked Elisha, in II Kings 2:9-13 [AMP],

*"...Ask what I shall do for you before I am taken from you. And Elisha said, I pray you, let a double portion of your **spirit** be upon me. He said, you have asked a hard thing. However,*

if you see me when I am taken from you, it shall be so for you; but if not, it shall not be so. As they still went on, and talked, behold, a chariot of fire and horses of fire parted the two of them; and Elijah went up by a whirlwind into Heaven. And Elisha saw it, and he cried, my father, my father!.. He took up also the mantle of Elijah..."

The Bible records that Elisha did twice as many miracles as Elijah; he did indeed receive the spirit (mantle, anointing) of Elijah in double portion as he had believed. Many years after his death, a man was even raised from the dead just by coming into contact with Elisha's bones!

A New Testament example of the transfer of an anointing is the Apostle Paul and his son in the Lord, Timothy. No other man was as faithful to serve Paul and learn from him as Timothy. In writing to the Philippian church, Paul says of Timothy in Philippians 2:19-22 [AMP],

*"But I hope and trust in the Lord Jesus soon to send Timothy to you, so that I may also be encouraged and cheered by learning news of you. For I have no one like him – no one of so **kindred a spirit** – who will be so genuinely interested in your welfare and devoted to your interests. For the others all seek [to advance] their own interests, not those of Jesus Christ, the Messiah. But Timothy's tested worth you know, how as a son with his father he has toiled with me zealously [serving and helping to advance] the good news (the Gospel)."*

Because Timothy associated so closely with Paul and actively sought to learn from him, a mantle of Paul's ministry and anointing rested upon Timothy. Paul could send Timothy as his ambassador knowing that he would not misrepresent him or the Lord.

The Dangerous Transference of Spirits

Even as Paul desired to raise up others in the faith that could carry on and expand upon his work to spread the Gospel, I want to see young men and women raised up at the Eagle's Nest who can minister the Gospel over the entire earth. One such young man is Eric, now one of my staff pastors. Eric was saved at the Eagle's Nest seven years ago. He spent much of his early life searching for God in Eastern religions, psychic phenomenon, and rock music. But he desperately wanted to know a god who was real and had power, not the one portrayed in the dead religion he had seen in so many conventional Christian churches. After a startling dream in which God spoke directly to him, his praying mother convinced him to visit the Eagle's Nest where he made a firm decision to serve God and turn away from his old, carnal life-style. In obedience to His new master, Jesus Christ, he destroyed the books, rock albums, and occultic paraphernalia from his past and turned to follow Jesus completely.

Almost immediately, he began faithfully attending Bible classes. In his zeal, he attended every service and function of the church and soon found areas where he could serve the church and others. Later, he became an intern pastor and began to serve as a worship leader in some of the services. As a worship leader in the music ministry, he had learned how to "flow" with me in ministry. Now, as a staff pastor, Eric has taken on more and more of my mantle, ministering in the gifts much as I do. Even though he never purposed to minister like me, there has been a transference of anointing from me to him. Although he teaches and preaches with a similar anointing to mine, God has given him his own style and emphasis.

I believe God has entrusted him with a similar mantle because of his submissive and humble spirit.

Have you ever noticed how young ministers raised up under a senior minister, begin to talk, walk, act, and even take on the mannerisms of their senior? I believe they receive mantles of anointing and gifts through transference.

Family Ties of Transference

There can even be a transfer of anointings through the family line. The Old Testament high priesthood was passed through the line of Aaron and only those who were biological members of the tribe of Levi could serve as priests. Zechariah 1:1 tells us that the prophet Zechariah was a third generation prophet like his father and grandfather before him. The faith that was found in Timothy had also been seen in his mother Eunice and his grandmother Lois, according to II Timothy 1:5.

To illustrate another remarkable instance, Steve Gleason, a young minister working in the movie and television industry, shared how the famous third world evangelist, T. L. Osborne, transferred his mantle to Gary Osborne, his nephew, on one occasion. About fourteen years ago, Gary was working with the Osbornes to set up crusades and help in their follow-up. On a particular crusade, T. L. became ill and was unable to speak to the 200,000 anxiously awaiting people who had gathered to hear him. Even though Gary had never ministered to such a large group, T. L. asked him to fill in for him and share the same kind of "simple gospel message" he had preached all those years. He instructed him to pray a simple prayer, count to ten, and expect miracles to flow before he reached ten.

With much trepidation, Gary Osborne obediently preached the simplest gospel of Jesus Christ he knew. Then he told the people he would pray that the devil would be bound, and that as he did so, the blind would begin to see, the deaf would hear, the cripples would walk, and the demonized would be set free. He closed his eyes and began counting for what seemed the longest ten seconds of his life.... But as he reached seven, he suddenly opened his eyes as people began screaming. Blind eyes were opened, deaf ears began to hear, and cripples were walking! As Gary watched the canes being thrown into the air and people rising from their stretchers, he thanked and praised God even as he breathed a great sigh of relief.

There are numerous modern examples of the transfer of anointings. Out of the Salvation Army, begun by William Boothe, came the great evangelists Gypsy Smith, Smith Wigglesworth, Howard Carter, and George Jeffreys, just to name a few. John G. Lake worked with John Alexander Dowie and received an incredible healing mantle from him. Kenneth Copeland carried Oral Roberts' suitcase and served him faithfully before beginning his own ministry while Jerry Savelle assisted Kenneth Copeland before the Lord trusted him with his own ministry, and so on.

A dear friend of mine and prophet of God, Dr. Bill Hamon, shared with me at dinner one night that out of twenty eight people (including his own family) who have spent time in his household, all have received strong spiritual mantles for prophesying.

Different Strokes for Different Folks

For years I have been questioning the amazing transference of strife and division I have seen erupt in families and churches over and over. For instance, several years ago a church in financial trouble deeded their whole property over to the Eagle's Nest Christian Fellowship. It seemed like a tremendous opportunity for both our church people and that church body... until disagreement, divisions, and malicious stories started circulating. Nothing we did for them made them happy, and none of the pastors or musicians from the Eagle's Nest that we sent to minister in that church pleased their people. Finally, a lawsuit, falsely accusing the Eagle's Nest of taking their property, was filed by one of the former board members of that church. The Eagle's Nest board of directors and elders had to face a difficult, but inescapable fact. The other church members had another spirit from that of the Eagle's Nest. Their goals, vision, emphasis, and desires were completely different from those of the Eagle's Nest.

Although we finally managed to free the Eagle's Nest from any further obligations to that church, it was not before the spirit of that other church had adversely affected some of our members who had spent time ministering there. I saw that some of the gossiping, bitterness, division, and strife that characterized that church body was infiltrating our people at the Eagle's Nest like seeds of cancer. Even though we broke all association with them, the spirit they transferred to us eventually caused a violent church split.

Jesus said, in Matthew 12:25,

> *"...Every kingdom divided against itself is brought to desolation; and every city or house divided against itself shall not stand."*

When someone comes from one church to another, often they do not agree with the vision and goals of the new church. Sadly, they do not understand that even though different ministries and churches have different goals, different visions, and different emphases does not make one right and another wrong. God has placed differences in His body so that we can meet different needs and complement one another, not compete with one another. Just as there are different callings on individuals, churches also have special callings. One ministry might emphasize deep worship, healing, and pastoral care; another might be more directed toward teaching and mission outreach; and another might specialize in prophecy, the end-times, and restoration. It is important for every Christian to be a part of a church body that has a similar calling and spirit to his. If a Christian attends a church where he does not feel a kindred spirit or he feels the emphasis is wrong, he may be the "little leaven that leavens the whole lump." In other words, he may sow strife and disunity in that body by his different views. Everyone in a church has to have the same vision, the same goals, and the same direction in order for there to be a unity of purpose. It is only when there is unity of spirit that the power of God is seen in a church body.

I attended a church many years ago where several of the elders and associates began to murmur about the pastor's overemphasis on the book of Revelations. As they talked about the situation among themselves, a spirit of disunity and discontent entered the church. The complaints spread among the leadership until a secret meeting was called at a local restaurant where everyone could discuss a remedy. A spokesman was chosen from the group to rebuke the pastor. Since I was involved, I must admit that we did not take into account I Timothy 5:1, which says,

"Rebuke not an elder, but entreat him as a father..."

There were three courses we should have taken to prevent falling into error. First, we should not have discussed our feelings and observations among ourselves in secret. Instead, we should have gone individually to the pastor as our spiritual father and lovingly shared our concerns with him. Secondly, we should have prayed individually and asked God to deal with him and show him his error. And thirdly, if we were not satisfied, we should have sought out another church with whose spirit we felt unity. We were of a wrong spirit even though we may have been right about some of our issues of concern!

It is imperative that the leadership of a church all have the same spirit, the same vision, the same goals, and the same attitudes as the head pastor. A church with divided leadership, each one pulling the people in different directions, will not flourish for long. Several years ago the Eagle's Nest experienced an agonizing split because we had brought in several pastors from the outside with very good qualifications, but different spirits and visions from ours. Disagreement caused us to be a house divided. When those men eventually left, over a thousand people also left. Since then God has rebuilt our church on a strong foundation with unity of spirit. Our leaders are now of one mind, one spirit, and one heart, and we are going forward together to fulfill the calling God has given us because we are submitted to one another.

Even though as Christians we all have the same Spirit of Christ within us, we manifest different aspects of God's Spirit. We need to fellowship in and be a part of a church body that has an emphasis we are in harmony with. I Corinthians 12:4-5 [AMP] says,

> *"Now there are distinctive varieties and distributions of endowments [extraordinary powers distinguishing certain Christians due to the power of divine grace operating in their souls by the Holy Spirit] and they **vary**, but the (Holy) Spirit remains the same. And there are distinctive varieties of service and ministration, but it is the same Lord [Who is served]."*

Wild Doctrines

Just as a different vision or calling can bring a spirit of disunity into a church, untried and unproven doctrines from the outside may bring a spirit of confusion and error into a church body. A young, zealous Christian may try to bring "new exciting revelations" he has heard through radio, television, or his Bible study into his church. In his enthusiasm, he may share them with his friends at church. He may bring confusion and strife, or even error, into the body because he does not fully understand these new doctrines and does not have the foundations in his life to carefully examine them in the light of the Word of God.

The Apostle Paul warns us about what can happen when someone comes into a church with new "revelation." II Corinthians 11:3-4 says,

> *"But I fear, lest by any means, as the serpent beguiled Eve through his subtlety, so your minds should be corrupted from the simplicity that is in Christ. For if he that cometh preacheth another Jesus, whom we have not preached, or if ye receive another spirit which ye have not received, or another gospel, which ye have not accepted, ye might well bear with him."*

In other words, Paul is fearful that they might be persuaded by a false teacher to accept error and another spirit other than the spirit of Christ!

Alexander William Ness shares a story of how his father's church was severely damaged by the introduction of "new revelations" by two traveling ministries in his book, **The Transference of Spirits.**

> *"My father pastored an evangelical church. One day, two traveling evangelist-teachers came to the church with "new light" and "deeper teaching." After consultation with several elders they allowed them into their church. They taught, sang and brought what seemed a revival in the church. Troubled in his spirit, my father expressed his concern to other elders but was overruled and the meeting went on for two months.*

The Dangerous Transference of Spirits

All-night prayer meetings developed into a very unhealthy situation. These two men were found guilty of immorality and fled the country, but their spirit remained and led to a complete split in the church. It has never recovered."[2]

The Bible warns that in the last days there shall be destructive seducing spirits in our churches....

II Kings 4:38-41 gives us a spiritual parable of wild doctrines or strange teachings being brought in from the outside without the leader's direction.

"And Elisha came again to Gilgal: and there was a dearth (scarcity of food) in the land; and the sons of the prophets (the young men being raised up under Elisha) were sitting before him: and he said unto his servant, set on the great pot, and seethe pottage (stew) for the sons of the prophets. And one went out into the field to gather herbs, and found a wild vine, and gathered thereof wild gourds his lap full, and came and shred them into the pottage: for they knew them not. So they poured out for the men to eat. And it came to pass, as they were eating of the pottage, that they cried out, and said, O thou man of God, there is death in the pot. And they could not eat thereof. But he said, then bring meal. And he cast it into the pot; and he said, pour out for the people, that they may eat. And there was no harm in the pot."

Notice that Elisha sanctioned one servant to prepare the food for the men. In our case, the pottage is symbolic of the word the anointed leader teaches us under God's direction – the teachings that are sanctioned. But in our parable, another one went outside of the camp who had not been sent by Elisha. He gathered wild, poisonous gourds and tried to feed the company of young prophets with them. The wild gourds represent poisonous, unproven teachings from outside the church (or camp) being mixed with the true teachings of the church. The story says, "...they knew them not." In other words, they were strange and contrary to the teachings of the church. The meal that Elisha cast into the situation represented the pure Word of God.... The only remedy to heal another spirit or poisonous teaching that infects the church is the pure Word of God.

Excess Baggage

Every leader may transfer both his positive and his negative qualities to his followers. Many times an influential leader or teacher will have some peculiar and unique personality traits which characterize him. These qualities are often negative and are tolerated in the individual only because of the special gifts he has to offer. However, the young men and women who are taught and nurtured by such a person may eventually acquire not only the good qualities of such a person, but also these negative traits.

Several years ago, I noticed some of my staff members, elders, and teachers were becoming very impressed and enamored by the teachings of a certain television and radio personality. While I did not necessarily believe this teacher had an evil spirit, he was well-known for being extremely verbal and having a negative attitude toward politicians, Christian leaders, government officials, and others. Even though this man had brought out many wonderful revelations from the Bible, his haughty, critical, and condescending attitude was very apparent to everyone. He even made a habit of calling those with opposing viewpoints degrading names in public. It was my belief that he had a wrong spirit.

I became very concerned for the members of my congregation who were being affected by the "excess baggage" of this man's character. His critical, haughty spirit was being transferred to them as they listened to and learned from his teachings. He definitely had another spirit that was diametrically opposed to the spirit of unity and love I was trying to foster in my church. I finally had to forbid the membership of the Eagle's Nest from listening to him if they were to continue to submit to our authority. It quickly became apparent how much that teacher's attitudes had affected some of my members as they resigned and left the church over my mandate.

Many times we allow individuals with another spirit in our churches, our businesses, and even in our homes because we feel they have so much to offer or perhaps they are related to us. But all the good that they do will invariably be negated many times over by the destructive transference of their different spirit. Paul warns in Galatians 5:9 [AMP],

> *"A little leaven (a slight inclination to error, or a few false teachers) leavens the whole lump [it perverts the whole conception of faith or misleads the whole church]."*

He is saying the leaven (or introduction) of another spirit will affect many others. This truth can apply to doctrines, attitudes, or even personality traits.

Ministries of Mixture

Sometimes the spirit of the world system looks so exciting and glamorous that we try to mix worldliness with the Word of God. The world says get success at any cost. We have all seen a spirit of greed among many leaders. They use "Madison Avenue" advertising and merchandising techniques to promote their "gospel" of success and prosperity. They often measure the success of a person's life by the material possessions he is able to acquire. But Jesus cautions us, in Luke 12:15,

> "... Take heed and beware of covetousness: for a man's life consisteth not in the abundance of the things which he possesseth."

There is nothing in itself wrong with having nice things and being affluent, but it has never been the measure of success for the Christian life nor should it ever be the goal of the Christian. Money for a Christian should only be a tool that enables him to do the will of God and frees him from the burden of struggling to exist and providing for those in his charge.

I have seen the great temptation for ministers and their followers to preach success, prosperity, and having the "best" rather than the denial of selfish desires and simple faith in Jesus Christ. When positive thinking, confession, prosperity, and success draw us away from daily, intimate fellowship with Jesus and daily Bible study and prayer, the spirit of the world is seducing us away from God. Let me show you the typical way satan, the angel of light as he is called in II Corinthians 11:14, seduces us away from our first love, Jesus. A man may begin very humbly, seeking God with all his heart. He spends his days in prayer and fasting and studying the Word of God. God blesses this man and rewards his diligence for Hebrews 11:6 says God is a rewarder of those who diligently seek Him. As God begins to pour His Spirit out upon such a man, people are drawn by the anointing and charisma of the Holy Spirit and the power of God in his life. Suddenly, he is very popular and people begin to look up to him and adulate him. As he becomes more popular, money pours in as people bless him and support his ministry. Often, he feels he must maintain a debonair, prosperous image with expensive clothes, jewelry, and styling.

The more popular he becomes, the less time he has available to spend seeking God. But his followers, for the most part, are not aware that the anointing has decreased because this man has now learned how to use his own charismatic personality to please and manipulate the crowd. In fact, he has adopted the world's way of success.... His hair is now carefully coiffured, his clothes are impeccably stylish, he drives an exquisite car, lives in the "best" neighborhood, and moves with the "right" crowd. He has followed the advertising promoter's advice to make sure his name and face are seen and heard everywhere – in magazines, on television, on radio.

But with his continued success and popularity comes the increased budget. Unfortunately, his superstar image also has a superstar price tag. He must now resort to fund-raising schemes and direct mail "squeeze the people" tactics. He even hires professional fund-raising and marketing specialists to help him solicit the ever-increasing funds needed to support his growing empire. Gradually, this once humble servant ends up promoting himself and his own ministry and popularity instead of Jesus Christ and *Him* crucified.

Tainted Techniques

Many large ministries have fallen into the mold of the spirit of this world which says the end justifies the means. They have developed fund raising methods that are based on emotional appeal and guilt rather than the Spirit of God moving on the hearts of His people. They send "disaster-grams" that say their ministry will go under unless a person sends his money today or that children will starve to death unless money is sent immediately. They bypass need in favor of desperate need; their letters are all superlatives. One well-known evangelist showed emaciated children with the caption, "By the time you read this, this child will probably be dead...." An even more pathetic reality is that much of the money raised by these questionable means never goes to the cause for which it was raised.

Paul, in anticipation of our struggle with the world system, warns us to judge our works whether they are for our own glory or the glory of God. He says in I Corinthians 3:13-15,

> *"Every man's work shall be made manifest; for the day (the day of judgment) shall declare it, because it shall be revealed by fire; and the fire shall try every man's work of what sort it is. If any man's work abide which he hath built*

thereupon, he shall receive a reward. If any man's work shall be burned, he shall suffer loss; but he himself shall be saved; yet so as by fire."

It is only in judging ourselves, that we can avoid the judgment of God, according to I Corinthians 11:31.

In another example, a man is seeking God with all his heart. He sacrifices everything to spend time with God and study the Word, but he has no regrets because of the sweetness of God's presence in his life. God meets him and begins to pour His spirit out on the man's life. He finds himself greatly used of God to bring deliverance, healing, and miracles into people's lives. But even as he is able to challenge others to faith and to receive the blessings of God, the spirit of the world creeps into his own life. You may well ask, how can that man be bringing others into the kingdom of God and be yielding to the spirit of the world at the same time?

When any man or woman is being mightily used by God, pride, a haughty attitude, and selfishness can gradually characterize their lives if they are not yielding fully to God's control. A man who is fully yielded to the Spirit of God will exhibit the fruits of the Spirit as his character traits – love, joy, faith, peace, patience, gentleness, goodness, meekness, and self-control (Galatians 5:22-23). If the spirit of the world is mixing with this man's spirit and not allowing the Holy Spirit to control his life, pride and haughtiness will often be evident.

Manipulation By Mammon

The lust for worldly power, possessions, and position compromises leaders every day. Let me share a scripture and an example of how a minister or leader may manifest the spirit of the world and the Spirit of God at the same time. Again, it comes down to the choice to which spirit a person yields. In Numbers, chapters 22-24, we are given the account of Balaam, a prophet of God. Numbers 23:5 tells us that God put a word in his mouth. In other words, God spoke through Balaam to the people. We also read about Balak, the king of the Moabites (the enemies of Israel), who represents satan and the tempting spirit of this world. Evil Balak knew that if he could convince Balaam to curse Israel, that nation would indeed be cursed. In Numbers 22:6, Balak says to Balaam,

> "... for I know that he whom thou blessest is blessed, and he whom thou cursest is cursed."

Balak offered Balaam worldly rewards and position if he would compromise his divine calling. In Numbers 22:7, Balak offered him rewards and prosperity and in Numbers 22:17, he offered him promotion, honor, and worldly popularity. When those enticements were not enough, Balak requested that Balaam accompany him to another site, "Pisgah," from where he could view Israel and his ministry from another perspective. It is interesting that this is the same mountain from which Moses viewed all of the promised land. Similarly, Luke 4:5-7 relates how satan also took Jesus to a high mountain to show Him the kingdoms of this world that would be His to rule if He would bow down and serve satan! Satan uses the same tactics, the lust of the eyes (things), the lust of the flesh (sensual pleasures), and the pride of life (power and glory) against *all* of us.

I am reminded of the minister who swept into California some time ago, boasting that he would have the largest church on the West Coast. With his charismatic personality and gifts, he quickly built a church of over eight hundred people. His business manager said that over seven hundred and fifty thousand dollars had been received as tithes and offerings by the church in its first year. Even though that minister was winning many souls to the Lord, there were some fatal flaws in his character. First, he felt he should be earning a salary of one hundred and four thousand dollars in his first year of ministering. Next, he bought a beautiful home costing two hundred and seventy nine thousand dollars which was located in one of the prime areas of California, and he expected the church to make all the payments. He also leased himself a gorgeous Mercedes.

There seemed to be an intoxication that overtook him as he increased in power and personal charisma. He began borrowing large sums of money from several people in his congregation so he could continue building his church kingdom. The sad part is that he made no effort to pay back any of those loans and even failed to pay his staff their salaries. To make matters worse, he had fallen into a rumored extramarital affair which caused many members of his church to leave.

SEDUCTIONS EXPOSED

The final crash of the church came when sixteen lawsuits were filed against him for more than a hundred thousand dollars. It would appear that his downfall came because the lust of the eye, – wanting all those beautiful things, the lust of the flesh, – wanting a relationship outside of his marriage, and the pride of life, – wanting the power and glory of having the biggest and the best overnight, – all had brought him to the loss of everything!

Remember that Balaam was a man of God just like this pastor, but he also had a free-will choice. He could have obeyed God and refused to fellowship with the enemy, but he played with temptation, stayed in Balak's court, and slowly received a lethal transference of worldliness and compromise. In spite of Balaam's failures, God continued to speak through him, using him again and again. But Balaam had become corrupted in his spirit – he loved money and material possessions and worldly power more than God. He was manipulated by mammon. Even though Balaam refused to curse Israel with his words, he found another way to destroy them for a reward. He told evil King Balak that if he could get them to fornicate with the women of Moab, leading them into idolatry, God Himself would punish the people of Israel for their own disobedience.

Later, to the church of Pergamus, Jesus says in Revelation 2:14 [AMP],

"Nevertheless I have a few things against you: you have some people there who are clinging to the teachings of Balaam, who taught Balak to set a trap and a stumbling-block before the sons of Israel, [to entice them] to eat food that had

been sacrificed to idols and to practice lewdness – giving themselves up to sexual vice."

The prophet had fallen so far from the ways of God that even though he still obeyed God with his words, his heart was far from Him!

The Apostle Peter referred to the error and doctrine of Balaam in II Peter 2:15-16, when he said,

> *"Which have forsaken the right way, and are gone astray, following the way of Balaam the son of Beor, who loved the wages of unrighteousness; but was rebuked for his iniquity: the dumb ass speaking with a man's voice forbad the madness of the prophet."*

Balaam could have listened the first time God spoke to him to forsake Balak and bless Israel, but he opened himself to compromise and in the end, he was rejected both by God and by men. Joshua 13:22 tells us that this backslidden prophet, or soothsayer as he was now called, was killed by the very men of Israel that he was once commanded to bless.

Just as God did not tolerate Balaam mixing the Word of God with the spirit of the world, He will not allow men of God to move in His anointing with hidden sins in their lives. The Christian musicians who travel about the country with girls in their bus, the pastor who rushes from the prayer meeting to another man's wife, and the evangelist who watches pornographic movies in his hotel room to relax after a crusade... all these hidden sins and secret lives are being revealed as God judges those who call themselves Christians. God's mercy and grace is long-suffering, but God will not continue to overlook sin in the lives of those who take His name as their own. God is demanding holiness from His people and separation from the spirit of the world. II Corinthians 6:17-18 commands,

> *"Wherefore come out from among them, and be ye separate, saith the Lord, and touch not the unclean thing; and I will receive you, and I will be a Father unto you, and ye shall be My sons and daughters, saith the Lord Almighty."*

Judge Thyself...

Today, as never before in history, all of us need to examine our Christian walk. If we realize that a spirit of worldliness and compromise has indeed crept into our Christian walk, let us repent of it, turn away from it, and seek the Lord with *all* our heart. Or, if we have allowed ourselves to come under the influence of someone or a group that is not of God, let us break that association and renounce any ungodly spirits that may have been transferred to us. I Corinthians 11:31 promises,

> *"For if we would judge ourselves, we should not be judged."*

If we continue to compromise and mix God's Spirit with the world's spirit, God's blessings and covering will finally cease and judgment will fall....

God *will* have a church that is holy and pure, a church that is filled with His spirit. Ephesians 5:25-27 says,

The Dangerous Transference of Spirits

...even as Christ also loved the church, and gave Himself for it; that He might sanctify and cleanse it with the washing of water by the Word, that He may present it to Himself a glorious church, not having spot or wrinkle, or any such thing; but that it should be holy and without blemish."

As Christians we are to be that church!

Hands on Experiences

We have dealt with transference of spirits by association, but in concluding this subject, let me briefly mention transference by impartation. There are numerous purposes for the laying on of hands in both the Old and New Testament scriptures, and there are examples of the laying on of hands for the transference of ministries, gifts, mantles, and anointings. When Moses laid hands on Joshua, his wisdom and his counsel came upon Joshua. Deuteronomy 34:9 says,

"And Joshua the son of Nun was full of the spirit of wisdom; for Moses had laid hands on him."

The Lord also took of the spirit that was upon Moses and put it on the seventy elders so they could share the burden of governing the people with Moses in the wilderness. Numbers 11:16-17 says,

"And the Lord said unto Moses, gather unto Me seventy men of the elders of Israel, whom thou knowest to be elders of the people, and officers over them; and bring them unto the tabernacle of the congregation, that they may stand there with thee. And I (the Lord) will come down and talk with thee

*there: and I will take of the **spirit** which is upon thee, and will put it upon them; and they shall bear the burden of the people with thee, that thou bear it not thyself alone."*

The governing of several million people was too much for Moses to handle alone, but God wanted them to receive the same kind of counsel that Moses would have given them. These seventy men supernaturally received the same spirit that Moses had so they could minister to the people with his wisdom, his mind, his vision, and his anointing.

In Acts 6:6, Stephen, Phillip, and others had hands laid on them as they were set in the office of deacons by the apostles for the purpose of serving the widows at tables. Later in verse 8, we read that Stephen was performing great wonders and signs in front of the people. I believe the apostles had transferred more to them than the ministry of serving tables – they had also transferred gifted ministries to them, including the working of miracles.

Several years ago I was attending a Bible study in the home of my friend Andy. Having been healed of back problems myself, God had given me faith for the healing of backs, and I felt led to impart this gift to Andy and others by the laying on of hands that night. In Romans 1:11, Paul states that he longs to see the Roman believers that he might impart spiritual gifts to them. Now Andy was a car salesman by trade and not what most people would consider a "spiritual" person or a likely candidate for a healing ministry. After I had laid hands on him and imparted the gifts of healings to him, almost everyone Andy prayed for that night was miraculously healed, and to this day, healings take place whenever he lays hands on the sick and prays in Jesus' name. He has even traveled with me and God has done mighty creative miracles through his hands. Andy not only received my gift through the laying on of my hands, but the Lord imparted the gift of faith to him.

There is also a negative and dangerous aspect of the laying on of hands which we must not ignore. In I Timothy 5:22, Paul warns Timothy,

> *"Lay hands suddenly on no man – (Do not be in a hurry in the laying on of hands [AMP]), neither be a partaker of other men's sins; keep thyself pure."*

Some teachers interpret this scripture to mean we must not impart gifts, callings, and ministries to men before their faithfulness and character are proven. If we prematurely lay hands on them in endorsement and impartation, then we are partakers with them in the sins they may commit.

The preceding scripture, verse 21, warns against showing partiality or preference to individuals. For instance, we might lay hands on a wealthy businessman to impart a leadership ministry to him because he has given thousands of dollars to the church. If his morals and integrity are lacking, we are responsible and partakers of his sins before God.

Another interpretation of being a partaker of other men's sins by the laying on of hands is that there might be an evil or sinful transference of a wrong spirit from one to another.

Even though I favor the first interpretation, I have seen too many examples of the second application to totally discount it. It appears there can be a negative transference received by the one laying hands on another, or a negative transference to the one having hands laid on them. For instance, recently a young Christian woman tearfully told me that she had experienced a traumatic encounter with a small group of intercessors in someone's home. Being a fairly new Christian, this young woman had found herself confused as one of the older women told her that she wanted to release a spirit of prophecy in her so she could give the older woman a prophetic word. The older Christian supposedly said, "I'll lay hands on you so you can prophesy to me for the Lord."

This young Christian woman submitted to the older, but was shocked by what followed. After laying hands on her, the older woman went on to inform her that she had received numerous prophecies concerning *her* upcoming marriage to a certain pastor. The older woman wanted more confirmation for this upcoming event so she asked the younger Christian to use her new gift to seek God and prophesy about the marriage.

The younger Christian was so confused that she ended up in my office depressed, disillusioned, and feeling manipulated. In fact, a spirit of oppression had followed her from that evening because she believed a wrong spirit had been released to her through the laying on of hands.

As this illustration clearly shows, it is dangerous to let just anyone lay hands on you in the name of spiritual experience unless you know their ministry is sound and above reproach. In I Thessalonians 5:12, Paul emphatically says,

> *"And we beseech you, brethren, to **know them** which labor among you, and are over you in the Lord, and admonish (exhort and warn you)..."*

A person who is deceived does not know he is deceived. A wolf can come in among the sheep and not know he is a wolf. That is why we must be careful that those who minister to us have the character of Jesus, not just His words!

SEDUCTIONS EXPOSED

SOUL TIES

Ties That Bind

I want to show you that through associations and relationships there might not only be a spiritual transference, but also a soulish transference and a soul tie formed between two people. A soul tie is the knitting together of two souls that can either bring tremendous blessings in a godly relationship or tremendous destruction when made with the wrong person. In fact, the stronger the soul ties, the more we become like those to whom we relate.

Sometime ago I was praying about a heartbreaking situation where the pastor of a large church had become driven by a spirit of adultery and lust. Even though he had a godly wife and children, he had become sexually involved with several of the young girls in his church. One of the girls realized he was using her when she saw him flirting with another young lady in the church. She left him for awhile, but found herself strangely in bondage to him emotionally and physically. She stayed away for awhile, but then he persuaded her to see him again. When she resumed the relationship, she became pregnant.... She is now raising her baby in our church.

Why did that young girl, who knew she was being used, find it so hard to break free of that pastor? How was she enslaved and in bondage to him? In II Corinthians 11:20, Paul laments, "For ye suffer it if a man brings you into *bondage*..." The Greek word for bondage, *kata dou lou*, literally means *enslaves you*. She had formed a strong soul tie to him through their sexual relationship; their souls had actually been joined together.

True Soul Brothers

A soul tie is a strong bond between two people in the realm of the soul. It can be either good or work for evil. An example of a good soul tie between friends is the story of Jonathan and David. Their souls were knit together. Knit means to tie together or join together. In I Samuel 18:1, it says,

> *"And it came to pass, when he (David) had made an end of speaking unto Saul, that the soul of Jonathan (Saul's son) was **knit** with the soul of David, and Jonathan loved him as his own soul."*

In verse 3, it goes on to say that David and Jonathan actually formed a covenant because they loved each other so deeply. Their souls were knit together; they were soul tied.

The stronger the bonding or soul tie between friends, the deeper and more lasting the relationship. The emotional and mental strength of one sustains the other in times of adversity and allows him to rejoice with the other in times of triumph. When the love between friends is pure and not polluted by any selfish desire, the bond between them works for good in their lives. Speaking of this kind of love, in John 15:13, Jesus said,

> *"Greater love hath no man than this, that a man lay down his life for his friends."*

In deep and true friendships like the one between Jonathan and David or even Ruth and Naomi, each party remains giving, faithful, and loyal even to his own hurt. Recognizing the divine call upon David, Jonathan gladly relinquished his right to inherit the throne of Israel to his friend. Similarly, Ruth gave up her own family and abandoned her homeland in order to follow and serve her mother-in-law, Noami.

Self-sacrificing soul ties like those between Jonathan and David or Ruth and Naomi form the basis of good marriages as well as enduring friendships. I heard of two young brothers who were so closely knit to each other that both were willing to make great sacrifices for the sake of the other. When they immigrated to America, they had no other means of support than to work at whatever menial jobs they could find. The one was well-built and industrious but not very bright while his brother was extremely intelligent, studious, and endowed with great potential to become a powerful lawyer. The not-so-bright brother offered to work in a run-down tenement building every day to support them both while his intelligent brother went to school and studied hard to become a lawyer. It was their agreement that after the one became prosperous as a lawyer, he would then support both of them. Because of their great love for one another, they fulfilled their agreement. They were so soul tied, committed, and willing to sacrifice that both brothers benefited from the relationship.

In deep and pure friendships and relationships, the two souls draw strength and encouragement from each other as well as security and love. In Ecclesiastes 4:9-12, Solomon describes the attributes of such a relationship. He says,

> *"Two are better than one; because they have a good reward for their labor. For if they fall, the one will lift up his fellow: but woe to him that is alone when he falleth; for he hath not another to help him up. Again, if two lie together, then they have heat: but how can one be warm alone? And if one prevail against him, two shall withstand him."*

There is actually a multiplication of strength as two people join together in committed relationships. Deuteronomy 32:30 says that one can chase a thousand, but two can put ten thousand to flight. In Matthew 18:19, Jesus also said that if two agree on earth as touching any thing in prayer, their heavenly Father would give them their petition.

One reason the early church in Jerusalem was so explosive and experienced such power was that the people were completely unified. In fact, they were soul tied because Acts 4:32 says,

> *"And the multitude of them that believed were of **one heart** and **one soul**: neither said any of them that aught of the*

things which he possessed was his own; but they had all things in common."

Their bond of unity was so strong and their hearts were so pure that they even freely shared all their possessions with one another!

Ungodly Ties of Destruction

While a soul tie will develop between any two people who are open to one another, the strength of those soul ties depends upon how deeply involved with one another their hearts become. We can become soul tied to people we are related to, people we live and work with, people we associate with, and also people to whose leadership we submit. In fact, the unity we have with others is an expression of our soul ties to them. Since those we are soul tied or knit to are so influential and important in shaping our lives, we should carefully examine our relationships and friendships, including those with family members.

When a person who is bonded to another is governed by impure motives or the desire for selfish gain, the soul tie between them can enable that selfish one to manipulate and abuse the other. A person can actually control another through soul ties because the mind, will, and emotions of the two people are now open to one another. In ungodly relationships, these soul ties may place us in emotional and mental bondage to others and causing us to do and say things to our own hurt.

SEDUCTIONS EXPOSED

Exactly how dangerous and harmful these ungodly soul ties can be is illustrated in this interesting article entitled, "Woman Counsel May Be Mesmerized" from the **Long Beach Press Telegram,** on April 2, 1983. An inmate, William Timothy Kirk, was to be tried for fatally shooting two other inmates at the Bushy Mountain Penitentiary. A Knoxville lawyer's assistant, Mary Evans, was appointed by the court as counsel to Kirk. According to the article,

> *"The young lawyer who assertedly helped her convict-client escape at gunpoint from a doctor's office five days before his double-murder trial may be 'controlled psychologically' by the man, her boss said Friday... the incident appears to be a case of 'Stockholm syndrome', named for a hostage situation in Sweden in which the phenomenon was first described. James Beall, the senior attorney, said, 'It's a psychological and emotional thing where a very dominant individual can overpower the will of the other and develop a relationship' ...A person is controlled psychologically and under the power of another person."*

Because this female lawyer became emotionally tied to and in bondage to her convict-client, she actually participated in his crimes and violated the basic tenants of the legal profession of which she was a part. As Christians, we can see destructive soul ties and witchcraft operating in this incident.

Even in seemingly good relationships, ungodly soul ties can develop if those relationships are not in divine order. For example, while in-laws have been the brunt of countless marriage jokes, those jokes reveal a subtle truth that is a serious problem in many marriages. If the soul ties to parents are not broken when two people are united in marriage, conflict will eventually arise. It is not that the married couple is to have no relationship to their parents, but rather that the stronger tie must now be to the spouse, and other relationships must now have a lesser allegiance and influence. In fact, in any relationship an ungodly soul tie can potentially be established if that relationship is not under the lordship of Christ. God demands first place in our hearts, spouses are to be second, followed by children, family, friends, and associates. When our strongest soul tie is to God, there is a divine covering and protection that will enable us to withstand forming ungodly soul ties.

Flesh of My Flesh

A soul tie in the Bible can be described not only by the word knit, but also by the word cleave which, according to **Strong's Exhaustive Concordance,** means "to bring close together, follow close after, be attached to someone, or adhere to one another as with glue." God desires for us to be soul tied to Him through the covenant of salvation and fellowship. Deuteronomy 10:20 says,

> *"Thou shalt fear the Lord thy God; Him shalt thou serve, and to Him shalt thou **cleave**, and swear by His name."*

In I Corinthians 6:17, it clearly says that "he who is joined to the Lord is one spirit with Him." We also become joined in mind, which is part of the soul, with the Lord because I Corinthians 2:16 confirms that "we have the mind of Christ."

SEDUCTIONS EXPOSED

One of the highest forms of soul ties is formed in the marriage relationship. Two people become knit together in the soulish realm when they become *one flesh*. According to Genesis 2:24, God purposed,

> *"Therefore shall a man leave his father and mother and cleave unto his wife and they shall be one flesh."*

Adam confirmed this relationship when he said in Genesis 2:23,

> *"And Adam said, This (woman) is now bone of my bones and flesh of my flesh..."*

In other words, "This is my other self or part." It is noteworthy that when two pieces of wood are glued together, they will not break in the place where glued, but rather in a new place.

Yet the marriage relationship is a type or picture of a higher relationship – our relationship to the Lord. Isaiah 54:5 says,

> *"For thy Maker is thine husband; the Lord of Hosts is His Name; and thy Redeemer the Holy One of Israel; the God of the whole earth shall He be called."*

Just as two people become one through the marriage covenant, we also become one with the Lord through the covenant of salvation. In Ephesians 5:30,32, Paul says it even more clearly,

"For we are members of His (Christ's) body, of His flesh, and of His bones... This is a great mystery: but I speak concerning Christ and the church."

Sexual Snares

Just as our soul ties to the Lord make us one with Him, when two people become bonded together in marriage, they also become one. Their soul ties are so powerful that they may in time walk, talk, and act alike. When one starts a sentence, the other may finish it. They may even begin to look alike. In love, they absorb the best from each other; in strife, they absorb the worst from each other. Because these soul ties are so strong, the marriage covenant was never created to be broken. Divorce is particularly devastating because two intertwined souls have to be literally ripped and torn apart. The intermingled cords of each other's souls cannot be separated without inflicting deep wounds upon one another.

If you listen to covenant marriage vows, you will witness two people becoming soul tied through confession. However, the marriage bed is the final consummation of two people becoming one flesh and one soul. The soul tie formed through the sexual union of marriage is unique – man was created to have this bond with only *one* person!

God has made the sexual union to be whole being to whole being... spirit to spirit, soul to soul, and body to body. This union is the reason marriage is such a wonderful covenant. In the beginning when God created man in the garden of Eden, he took a part of the man to make the woman. The original language says that He actually made them and called their name adam. Their unity was so perfect that they had the same name. It was only after they sinned and a separation came between them and God, that the woman was called Eve and the man was called Adam.

Since the sexual union of marriage ties two souls as one, what do you think happens if a person commits fornication or adultery with another person outside of his marriage? Actually, his soul becomes mysteriously knit and tied to the other person also – they cleave together just as in marriage. The soul ties formed through illicit sexual involvement can be as strong and binding as those formed through the marriage covenant.

The legendary lover, Errol Flynn, was notorious for his many affairs. One of his lovers, Beverly Aadland told how she became involved with Flynn in **People Magazine,** October 17, 1988. As a teenager, she had been led to believe she was reading for a part in a motion picture at Flynn's home. Actually, he had planned to seduce her and had arranged for everyone to leave them alone. After Flynn raped her and realized she was a virgin, he felt remorse, but neither he nor Aadland could resist the powerful desire to be together from that time on. Even though she initially felt used and abused, Aadland thought she was in love and she became Flynn's constant companion and traveled with him until his death. They had become soul tied through that initial encounter.

Genesis 34:1-3, gives us an illustration of how fornication and immorality form soul ties,

Soul Ties

> *"And Dinah the daughter of Leah, which she bare unto Jacob, went out to see the daughters of the land. And when Shechem the son of Hamor the Hivite, prince of the country, saw her, he took her, and lay with her, and defiled her. And his soul **clave** unto Dinah the daughter of Jacob, and he loved the damsel and spake kindly unto the damsel."*

Actually, Shechem did not love Dinah. After raping her, he lusted for her because he had become soulishly tied to her and his soul longed for her. Even through the defilement of rape, their souls had been tied together. Verse 8 of Genesis 34 makes this clear as Hamor, Shechem's father, approached Jacob, Dinah's father....

> *"And Hamor communed with them saying, the soul of my son Shechem longeth for your daughter: I pray you give her to him to wife."*

Sexual involvement can form such entangling tentacles of soul ties that it is extremely difficult to break off a relationship. Have you ever heard the expression, "I've got you under my skin?" As a teenager I worked at a dairy with Chad, a pastor's son. Chad was promiscuous and often bragged about his sexual conquests. However, one of Chad's girlfriends was a sweet, moral girl who refused to go to bed with him. Frustrated over her reluctance, one day he overpowered and raped her. After that experience, she became mysteriously enslaved to him and constantly called him wanting to be with him – he was "under her skin" through a soul tie. Sadly, he quickly grew tired of her and discarded her.... She was no longer a challenge.

The earlier story of the pastor who had finally impregnated the young girl from his church also illustrates how difficult it is to break these soul ties. She needed help from people outside her environment in order to be set free. To indicate how strong these soul ties are, Genesis tells us that the desire of the woman shall be for her husband or for the mate who becomes her first soul tied partner (her first sexual partner). Genesis 3:16 says,

"...And thy desire shall be to thy husband, and he shall rule over thee..."

It grieves me to see women dominated by men who keep them away from God. One of the Christian girls at the Eagle's Nest works with a young girl who is very hungry for God. The Christian girl has invited her to church and told her about Jesus. The girl cries and wants to commit her life to the Lord, but she cannot.... She is involved with a boyfriend who does not want anything to do with the church or God. She is so tied to him physically and soulishly that she cannot get free. She is enslaved and in bondage to him.

Sexual Slaves

God designed the universe to function with natural and spiritual laws that bring freedom when obeyed, but bondage and destruction when broken and violated. Just as two souls can be knit or made to cleave together in a covenant relationship, they can also be tied or knit together to form bondage and enslavement. Sexual union was ordained by God to make two marriage partners one flesh before God, but promiscuous premarital and extramarital affairs can mysteriously tie one's soul to many partners.

Most individuals have no conception of how promiscuity outside of marriage scatters their souls and destroys their ability to commit to one partner. One of the purposes of marriage is to provide for the sexual needs of the two partners. The Bible tells the marriage partners that they are to be the continual fountain through which the other is satisfied... a cistern not to be shared with others. Proverbs 5:15,17-19 says,

> *"Drink waters out of thine **own** cistern and running waters out of thine **own** well... Let them be **only** thine **own**, and not a strangers' with thee. Let thy fountain be blessed: and rejoice with the wife of thy youth. Let her be as the loving hind and the pleasant roe; let **her** breasts satisfy thee at all times; and be thou ravished (satisfied) always with **her** love."*

But what happens if one of the partners cuts off that fountain of sexual satisfaction to his mate? Often the mate is strongly tempted to seek sexual fulfillment elsewhere.

Many years ago before I entered the ministry and was still operating my sign company, I would take sign renderings to a certain architectural firm in a nearby city. I found the secretary of the firm very attractive and was elated when she agreed to have lunch with me one day. My hopes for a relationship were totally dashed when she informed me she was married. She said she loved her husband very much so I was perplexed as to why she was out with me. She explained that her husband who was a rock singer was constantly away on the road and she craved companionship. With great disappointment, I told her that my Christian ethics would not allow me to go out with a married woman.

The Apostle Paul understood that when a person feels deprived of his due marital rights, he may subconsciously seek out another partner to supply his sexual needs. In I Corinthians 7:5 [AMP], Paul warns,

> *"Do not refuse and deprive and defraud each other (of your due marital rights), except perhaps by mutual consent for a time, that you may devote yourselves unhindered to prayer. But afterwards resume marital relations, lest Satan tempt you [to sin] through your lack of restraint of sexual desire."*

When someone feels like they are dying inside of thirst for sexual fulfillment, they may suddenly feel alive again when they find another sexual partner. Often they do not even feel guilty at first. (Eventually, they will feel guilty if their conscience has not been dulled by continual sin.) At first they *reason,* "It's so good to be alive again.... I can't feel guilty.... How can this be wrong?... If this is such a sin, I should feel guilty and condemned...."

It is so easy to justify adultery when it seems to renew your zest for life, when your talents are coming alive again, and when there seems to be an excitement in seeing this strange new lover. Often a man assumes the new woman must be the woman he was meant to have all along and that he married the wrong person. But what he really needed was to have the excitement and fulfillment of love rekindled with his own wife. While there is usually a reason for adultery, it is *never* justifiable, and it is *always* sin.

The tragedy is that few people understand the incredible consequences of the supposedly casual affair. In I Corinthians 6:16, 18, Paul challenges,

> *"What! Know ye not that he which is joined (sexually) to an harlot (a sexual partner outside of marriage) is **one body** with her? For two, saith He (God), shall be **one flesh.** ...Flee fornication. Every sin that a man doeth is without the body; but he that committeth fornication sinneth against his own body."*

Because he has joined himself body, soul, and spirit to another, such a person is soul tied and "one flesh" with his sexual partner. As we have seen, this will work for either blessing or destruction.

You may be involved or becoming involved in a sexual relationship right now. You may justify what you are doing by saying, "We are different. We *really* love each other. We have made a commitment to each other. We plan to marry someday." But God says it is *sin* and it will bring eventual destruction and not blessing to your life. God never makes exceptions to His laws for you or anyone else! Romans 11:16 states,

> *"For if the first fruits (start or beginning) be holy, the lump is also holy: and if the root be holy so are the branches."*

A relationship begun in righteous and holy actions will often bring forth blessed and holy branches. On the other hand, a relationship begun in sin and fornication will many times bring forth evil branches and fruit. This could include adulterous cheating, divorces, and even children that indulge in immorality.

Buy Now...Pay Forever

It is because of the awesome strength of the physical union between a man and a woman that God warns us in Proverbs 5: 20,22,

> *"Why wilt thou, my son, be ravished with a strange woman; and embrace the bosom of a stranger? For the ways of a man are before the Lord, and He (God) pondereth all his goings. His own iniquities (sex sins) shall take the wicked himself, and he shall be holden (enslaved, tied) with the* **cords** *of his sins."*

The consequences of a casual affair can be harmful and enduring. The soul ties formed can actually bind a person for life. For instance, God has so built every woman that the first man who has sexual relations with her takes a form of dominion over her (Genesis 3:16). Her human spirit and soul is built to respond to the man by nurturing him, supplying affection to him, and being that man's fountain of satisfaction and blessing all through his life.

Some time ago I received a letter from Mary, a young woman whose story illustrates this truth in a very profound way. As a teenager in high school, she had gone steady with Dan. Even though Mary was not a Christian, she was a moral young woman and wanted to stay pure for her future husband. However, after being steadily pressured, she reluctantly entered into sexual relations with Dan. He told Mary that because they were so much "in love," sex was the natural response to express that love, and besides, "they would marry someday anyway." Mary became a Christian during her senior year and told Dan she could no longer have sex with him outside of marriage. She tried to win him to the Lord, but it soon became apparent that he wanted no part of the Lord and the Christian life-style.

After high school Mary and Dan broke off their relationship, and Mary moved away, hoping to leave Dan and all the memories of their relationship far behind. After some time, Mary fell in love with Bill, a wonderful Christian man, and eventually married him. The honeymoon of their marriage was wonderful but after that time, she began fantasizing about Dan even though he lived in another city and she had not seen him since several years before her marriage. She loved her husband, but strangely, felt an intense desire to see Dan and be with him. She could not understand her feelings to be with Dan because she no longer loved him. Even though she had repented of her fornication and even confessed it to her husband, her soul could not forget Dan and longed to be with him. The desire to see him became so intense that Mary feared to return to her former city even though her family still lived there. She was afraid to see Dan – afraid she could not resist the drive to physically give in to him.

When Mary was shown that her soul was tied to Dan's soul because he was her first sexual partner, she and her husband broke those soul ties in prayer. With the help of a forgiving and understanding husband, Mary was set free from bondage, healed, and emotionally enabled to give herself entirely to her husband. Her relationship with her husband is now better than ever and she no longer thinks of Dan or has any desire to see him.

I was told recently that in the province of Aquila, Italy, there are small villages where it has been the tradition for the newly married wives to sleep with the village priest on their wedding night. This outrageous tradition was instituted after one of the priests supposedly received a revelation from God instructing them to do so, but it is easy to see why these priests have perpetrated this tradition. There is an insidious consequence of this perverted practice.... It has been reported that in those villages the wives are always sneaking away from their husbands to see the priests. Why? Their first sexual relationships were with them; they had become soul tied to the priests. A mysterious covenant had been made between the women and the priests – the two had become "one flesh" just as God's Word declares.

God made women to develop a longing desire for their first lover (supposedly their husbands). Remember, in Genesis 3:16, God said to Eve,

> *"...And thy desire (or longing) shall be to thy husband, and he shall rule over thee."*

Realizing this, you can see why in II Timothy 3:6 [AMP], Paul says women can be led captive by unscrupulous men (playboy hedonists),

> *"For among them are those who worm their way into homes and captivate silly and weak-natured and spiritually*

Soul Ties

dwarfed women, loaded down with [the burden of their] sins, [and easily] swayed and led away by various evil desires and seductive impulses."

The dominion a soul tie gives a man over his lover is often so binding that he can insult and mistreat her but she seems helplessly enslaved to him. She can be verbally and physically abused, and yet she is unable and often unwilling to leave. Often, even if she does manage to leave such a man, she finds herself compelled to return to him.

Lucy, one of the young women in my church recently shared with me how she had been in bondage to a young man when she was in her late teens and early twenties. Since they worked together, they began their relationship as friends. But one day, a powerful physical attraction ignited between them, and they began to see each other on a regular basis. Soon they were living together. As their relationship progressed, he began to verbally abuse Lucy. He would tell her she was worthless, useless, ugly... things that utterly destroyed her self esteem. Lucy thought she loved him and wanted his love and affection more than anything else. Even when he would cast her aside, she would crawl back to him as soon as he would change his mind and desire her again. Because she was wanted one day and refused the next, she became an emotional cripple. Soon she stopped eating and started losing weight.

This naive, young woman believed everything her handsome, articulate lover said to her, including that she was the only woman in his life. When Lucy discovered later that he had consistently lied to her; that he had been involved with an older woman for many years; and that he had other women on the side from time to time, she was devastated. She tried to leave him, but was never able to stay away for very long. They were soul tied, and because those ties were so strong he was able to manipulate and control her almost at will.

During this time a friend of Lucy's became a Christian. She immediately began praying and believing for Lucy's salvation and would share the gospel with her at every opportunity. At her home one day, Lucy accepted Jesus Christ as her Saviour and Lord and also received the baptism in the Holy Spirit. Although she was still physically involved with the young man, she no longer lived with him. As she began to grow in the Lord, He gradually began to remove things from her past life-style. One day the Lord told her to completely break off the relationship and she obeyed. However, the emotional attachments were not so easily severed. It was only through the consistent prayers and counsel of her friend that Lucy was able to regain her freedom. Still, it was two full years before she was fully restored emotionally, mentally, and physically from the trauma of that destructive and binding relationship!

As we have examined the potentially destructive and binding power of soul ties, it is not hard to understand the supposed "fatal attractions" that can be formed in sexual and intimate relationships. Recently, a very popular and successful movie called **Fatal Attraction** depicted a woman who after a short affair with a married man developed such a fixation to him emotionally that her whole life became consumed with trying to possess him for herself. She went to such extremes as threatening him, trying to ruin his marriage, and even attempting to get him fired at work when he would not leave his wife and continue the affair. According to the March 20, 1989, cover story of **People Magazine,** a real-life fatal attraction may have occurred between actress Sean Young and actor James Woods. After their short-lived, but intense sexual affair, Woods broke it off and resumed his relationship with his former fiancé. The jilted actress has since been accused of sending hate-mail, pictures of dead animals, and even a bloody, mutilated doll to Woods and his fiancé. The situation became so serious that police were called in to investigate and a harassment suit has been filed by Woods against Young. In light of our discussion of the entangling web that can come from sexual soul ties, we can see how such a fatal attraction is very possible.

Scattered Souls

What do you think happens to people who have formed soul ties with *many* people through fornication and promiscuity? In reality, their souls have become fragmented and scattered among all their sexual partners. They are unable to give themselves fully to their mates. Their thoughts and emotions are being continually drawn back to their past lovers.

John Sandford of Elijah House Ministries explained it from his perspective during a marriage seminar,

"If a woman has sexual relations with several men, her spirit and soul seek out every one of them. Her spirit is scattered and torn apart. A man's spirit is so built that for each woman he enters, his spirit is built to find, protect, bless, nurture and provide for that woman."[3]

A man's soul can also be scattered and destroyed through adulterous relationships. As Proverbs 6:27-29,32 clearly says,

*"Can a man take fire in his bosom, and his clothes not be burned? Can one go upon hot coals, and his feet not be burned? So he that goeth to his neighbor's wife; whosoever toucheth her shall not be innocent... But whoso committeth adultery with a woman lacketh understanding: he that doeth it **destroyeth** his own soul."*

There is nothing more destructive than sexual promiscuity. I Corinthians 6:18 says,

"Flee fornication. Every sin that a man doeth is without the body; but he that committeth fornication sinneth against his own body."

Not only are the souls of persons who have been promiscuous drawn to all their former lovers, but when they marry they often have sexual and communication problems with their mates. They are unable to be sexually satisfied by their marriage partner because they suffer from a scattered soul and cannot share themselves fully with their mate. They often seek satisfaction, not only with multiplied partners, but also through experimentation with bizarre forms of sex that may eventually lead to perversion.

A friend recently shared the sad story of how her brother's soul became scattered, eventually shattering his life. As a young boy, Dave had made a habit of watching his aunt shower through a small hole in the wall of her basement apartment. He actually became addicted to watching her and formed a soul tie to her through this experience. It seems his aunt was also aware of his voyeurism and actually enjoyed and encouraged it. Later, at age eleven she had taken him on a shopping expedition during which she deliberately took him with her into a dressing room and undressed in front of him. These events and his unnatural soul tie to his aunt opened a door for a consuming lust to come into his life. As he grew into a young man, lust began to control his life... not just a lust for women, but also a lust for power, a lust for wealth, a lust for alcohol, and a lust for drugs.

When Dave tried to marry, his lusts always ended up destroying the relationships. Because he began frequenting prostitutes, he had formed so many soul ties that he could never give himself completely to one person, causing his relationships to end in frustration and failure. His many soul ties from the past were constantly pulling him apart so that his soul eventually became scattered and fragmented. It weakened his character and every aspect of his life to the point that he could not resist temptation. His passions were so consuming that evil spirits drew him into multiple relationships with loose women wherever he went.

When Dave became born again and a Spirit-filled Christian, he finally married. But he was still vulnerable to lust because his past soul ties had never been broken and his soul cleansed from his sexual sins. He had been unwilling to let go of his lustful memories and continued to fantasize about the women in his past. After a few months of marriage, Dave met another woman with exactly the same background as his. She had also accepted the Lord as her saviour and been baptized in the Holy Spirit. But, she also had been unwilling to cleanse the past and let go of her lustful passions. When they met, they almost immediately became involved in an adulterous affair and a powerful soul tie followed. After a short time, not only did their marriages end, but their affair also ended in mutual hatred.

Sadly, to this day although both their lives have become poisoned in every area, and they struggle just to maintain life and health, still, they are unwilling to repent. They seem oblivious to the potential destruction that James 1:14-15 [AMP] warns about,

> *"But every person is tempted when he is drawn away, enticed and baited by his own evil desire (lust, passions). Then the evil desire, when it has conceived, gives birth to sin, and sin, when it has matured, brings forth death."*

The reason their past soul ties were never broken is that they had never made a decision to deal with the past, break those ties, and let go of the emotional attachments, memories, and fantasies. Their multiplied soul ties had weakened their characters, their wills, their emotions, and their minds to the point that a decision to be free was extremely difficult to make. Proverbs 6:32 asserts,

> *"But whoso committeth adultery (or sex sins)... **destroyeth**
> **his own soul."***

Lust and sin *is* gratifying for the moment – but a person always pays later in shame, guilt, humiliation, anger at self, anger at God, sorrow, and torment. It is often difficult for a person heavily involved in lust and self-gratification to see that he is only deceiving himself in the name of "cheap thrills." Because such a person often lives in a world of denial, he cannot admit that he has done anything wrong in his sordid past. In his mind, there is no sin from the past to deal with and he does not want to change his future. He is unwilling to make a *decision* to change his life because he is actually addicted to lust. Years of sin have weakened his character to the point of destroying his desires for good and making his decision to change extremely difficult.

However, the good news is that no matter how far into sin and lust a person has fallen, with the help of the Lord, someone who has decided to serve the Lord with *all* his heart can be set free. One of the women in the Eagle's Nest, Laura, is a shining example of someone who has been set free from heavy sexual and drug bondage. Although Laura was raised in a Christian home and accepted the Lord as her saviour at an early age, her home-life was far from perfect. At about age eight, her father approached her and suggested they have sexual relations. Even though they never did have intercourse, Laura's trust was broken and rebellion towards all authority, including God, entered her heart.

Early in her teens, Laura entered into an incestual relationship with her brother and several of her cousins, opening the door further to a spirit of lust. At the same time, she started experimenting with drugs and alcohol trying desperately to cover the guilt, shame, and anger that was building in her heart. As Laura began to develop into a young woman, she first reacted frigidly to young men, but later became very promiscuous. She even started having emotional longings for another woman, but caught herself before she fell into a lesbian affair.

At age 23, she married a man she had been living with for some time, but found herself unable to remain faithful to the relationship. Both she and her husband were heavy drug and alcohol users and both had numerous affairs. By this time Laura was not only addicted to cocaine and heroin but had also turned to prostitution in order to pay for her drug habits. Unable to live any longer in the horrible pit into which she had fallen, Laura finally cried out to the Lord for help. During all those years of sin she was conscious of Jesus and felt His love reaching out to redeem and call her back to Himself. But because of her rebellious heart, she waited until life had become completely intolerable before she was willing to give up her lusts. In His mercy the Lord heard and answered her desperate cry!

With the help of her family and a support group, and by staying away from her old friends and environment, the Lord set her free from the drug and alcohol habits. The Lord also led her to the Eagle's Nest where she received counseling and began the process of restoration and healing. Laura's soul had literally been plundered and scattered through all the sexual and ungodly soul ties of her past. But as all those ties were broken through prayer, and as she forgave each person who had wronged her, she became more free and more complete in her soul. Her countenance even changed, and she began to radiate the love of Jesus.

Although at times Laura still has occasional memories that she has to cleanse with the blood of Jesus, the incidence of those memories has become less and she is no longer tormented by thoughts of the past. For the first time, she has learned to love her husband without feeling lust for others. For Laura the road to freedom from sexual bondage and lust has not been easy, but she has determined to stay faithful to the Lord and to keep her covenant to Him. He has kept her, and He has been continually restoring her. The Lord is even using her to minister to others who are in drug and sexual bondage.

Sexual Transference

So far, I have shown you how the soul of a person can be scattered through sexual relationships outside of the marriage covenant, but I also want to explain that there may be another very devastating and costly consequence of fornication. Remember that in I Corinthians 6:18, Paul writes that every sin is outside the body, but he who commits fornication sins against his own body. Almost in disbelief, Paul asks the church in I Corinthians 6:15-17,

SEDUCTIONS EXPOSED

"Know ye not that your bodies are members of Christ? shall I then take the members of Christ, and make them members of a harlot? God forbid. What? know ye not that he which is joined to a harlot is one body? for two, saith He, shall be one flesh."

Because the Christian is one with Christ, Paul is shocked and dismayed that someone would even dare to defile himself with an unholy, adulterous relationship.

Now here is the other consequence. As two people become one flesh through sexual intercourse, there may also be a transference of evil spirits (as we have seen).

Quite often in counseling homosexuals, I have learned that their desires for someone of the same sex were the direct result of a homosexual molestation as a child or in their adolescence. I believe, while they were in that uniquely vulnerable developmental time, the spirit of homosexuality was transferred to them through that initial sexual molestation. That spirit then actually began to draw others to itself. The spirit of homosexuality is such a strong spirit that few are able to break free of its slavery without spiritual and emotional help. I believe homosexuals are strongly, sometimes irresistibly, drawn to each other by the spirits working in them.

A friend recently shared how her uncle was molested by his brother at about eight years of age. Even though he married and determined to live a normal, heterosexual life-style, he was unable to do so. Eventually, both he and his wife had that same spirit of homosexuality oppressing them because of the transference of spirits through their marital soul tie. Neither of them were able to remain faithful to one another and after fourteen years they dissolved their marriage. The wife left for another woman and he for another man. This man also later molested his niece, and his lover recently molested the five year old son of another relative. The cycle of molestation and homosexuality is being transferred from generation to generation in that unfortunate family! I believe much of what we blame on heredity is nothing more than a transference of evil spirits (of both diseases and evil traits) down through the family line. These spirits operating down through the family generations are called familiar spirits.

Homosexuality is not the only spirit that may be transferred through sexual unions. Greed, unfaithfulness, lust for power and wealth, and many other ungodly spirits may transfer from one person to another.

Over and over I have observed seducing spirits assigned to bring the downfall of Christian leaders. Most pastors, whether married or single, can usually tell horror stories of women who have literally thrown themselves at them. Those leaders do not have to be physically good-looking, charming, or even financially well-off. The women being used to bring their downfall are actually driven by seducing spirits who have been assigned by satan to attempt to stop the preaching of the gospel and the work of God. Satan knows he cannot attack those men unless he can get them to break their own hedge of protection. So he sends beautiful women, whom he has already defiled with seducing spirits, to attempt to lure them into compromise. If he can manipulate those leaders into a sexual soul tie, he may freely transfer all manner of defiling and driving spirits to them and destroy the work of their ministry.

Restoration for Scattered Souls

I have truly come to appreciate God's laws and commandments. They are for our good – to keep our souls from being scattered among many lovers and to keep us from becoming the habitation of evil spirits. Psalm 119:1 says,

> *"Blessed are the undefiled in the way, who walk in the **law** of the Lord."*

Even when we have become scattered and defiled, God's Word shows us the way to deliverance and restoration. According to Psalm 19:7,11 [AMP],

> *"The law of the Lord is perfect, restoring the [whole] person...Moreover by them is Your servant warned [reminded, illuminated and instructed]; and in keeping them there is **great reward**."*

The deceived, hedonistic, and playboy philosophers would have you believe that "practice makes perfect," but not under God's laws! God values innocence and purity. According to Philippians 2:15,

> *"That ye may be blameless and harmless (innocent), the sons of God, without rebuke, in the midst of a crooked and perverse nation, among whom ye shine as lights in the world."*

But God can take even those who have been shattered and defiled through sexual and worldly involvements and restore them to innocence and purity through the redemptive work of Jesus on the cross!

So what do we do if we are soul tied and mysteriously bound to many past lovers? The good news is that through the prayer of binding and loosing according to Matthew 18:18, we can be set free from those soulish ties to the past.... As you join me in the prayer of authority, we are going to uproot those tentacles of enslaving thoughts, emotional longings, and mystical sexual bondages to those in our past or outside our marriages. When we finish praying, I believe you will sense a new freedom and togetherness that will be truly miraculous. Your soul will be set on a path of restoration.

If you pray this prayer with me, believe and expect to be free of all ungodly soul ties. Do not pray insincerely or glibly. God promises to hear you when you come and seek Him with *all* your heart.

Pray In Faith, Receiving...

"Father, in the name of Jesus, I submit my soul, my desires and my emotions to your Spirit. I confess, as sin, all my promiscuous, premarital sexual relationships and all sexual relationships outside of marriage. I confess all my ungodly spirit, soul, and body ties as sin. I thank you for forgiving me and cleansing me right now!

"Father, thank you for giving me the keys of your kingdom, the keys of spiritual authority. What I bind is bound and what I loose is loosed. In Jesus' name, I ask you to loose me from all soulish ties to past sexual partners and ungodly relationships. Please uproot all the tentacles of sexual bondage, of emotional longings and dependencies, and of enslaving thoughts. I bind, renounce, and resist any evil spirits that have reinforced those soul ties or may have been transferred to me through evil associations.

"Please cleanse my soul and help me to forget all illicit unions so that I am free to give my soul totally to you and to my mate. Father, I receive your forgiveness for all past sex sins. I believe I am totally forgiven. Thank you for remembering my sins no more. Thank you for cleansing me from *all* unrighteousness. I commit myself totally to you. By your grace, please keep me holy in my spirit, soul, and body. I praise you. In Jesus' name, Amen!!!"

CHARISMATIC WITCHCRAFT

A Manipulating Influence

When a minister controls his congregation with fear and intimidation, this is witchcraft. When a father's continual anger and frustration adversely affects the mood and spirit of all his family members, this is a form of witchcraft. When a lonely housewife after studying positive thinking and mind power, begins to influence her husband at work to call home by meditating and asserting her will over him, this is witchcraft. Anyone who tries to use the power and Word of God to influence others in order to have his own selfish way is operating in charismatic witchcraft. I am using the term charismatic witchcraft to describe any *misuse* of spiritual or soulish power to manipulate and control others.

There is a classical witchcraft that is familiar to all of us in which a person influences and controls another person through amulets, spells, and potions, etc., with the aid of evil spirits. When we speak of witchcraft, we often picture an old woman with a wart on her nose, dressed in black, holding a black cat, and riding a broom. Most Christians would be horrified at the suggestion that God's children could operate in witchcraft, but Galatians 5:20, which was written to the Christians in Galatia, lists witchcraft as one of the works of the flesh. Assorted manifestations of witchcraft operate in every church in the world, especially in charismatic churches.

Have you ever noticed those in the church who act very "spiritual?" Often their speech will be filled with, "The Lord told me this... and the Lord told me that"... when it is clear from their lives that their direction is not from God at all. God seems to be in constant communication with them concerning even the smallest details of their lives. But these same "super-spiritual" people often try to manipulate others, they want to take control and have others looking to them as spiritual giants.

Just last night, I counseled a young man about some "super-spiritual" activities in which he was involved. He was absolutely convinced that a certain girl who sang in his church was called to be his wife, and he was doing everything in his power to make it appear that God was putting them together. The young girl asked me to counsel him because the pastors of the church they attended did not feel he was doing anything wrong. She had shared with me how he had written her and described a vision he had of them during a church service. Everyone in the room had supposedly disappeared while a light shone on the two of them, and "God" had spoken to him twice saying, "This is your wife." He soon began sending her letters, gifts, tapes, and messages through his friends telling her that it was God's will for them to be together.

This young man had convinced everyone in his church that he was very spiritual by frequently prophesying in the services, working in some of the departments of the church, and making himself available as a servant to the leadership. His pastors saw nothing wrong with his certainty that God had chosen the girl to marry him. My first indication that he was using manipulation and charismatic witchcraft upon the girl was that he had begun to pray for her will to line up with his. Secondly, he had stood in front of over a thousand people attending a church service and prophesied to her saying something like, "My daughter, my daughter, I've heard you singing unto Me in front of the multitudes but you have not yet been obedient and submitted in the issue I've spoken of. When you fully obey Me and submit, I'll set you free to minister in a glorious new anointing."

When I saw that the young man was using his spiritual gifts and influence to manipulate the young lady to become his mate, I shared with him that I believed that this was a working of his flesh. I told him that a familiar, seducing spirit was telling him she was to be his wife, stealing his peace and the peace of the young lady. His immediate response was that God had told him to send the gifts, letters, and to prophesy the words and that he had no choice but to obey God. I shared with him that I Corinthians 14:32 tells us that "the spirits of the prophets are subject to the prophets." In other words, God never gives a prophet a certain word and forces him to speak it. The grievous part of this story is that because he is such a spiritual young man, his leadership does not realize that he is misusing the gifts of God in trying to manipulate others around him and especially this young girl.

I want to show you that there is a form of charismatic witchcraft or fleshly manipulation that creeps into almost every church. Charismatic witchcraft uses the works of the flesh and a false spirituality to gain influence and power over others.

Before we examine this type of witchcraft in the church, let me share an example of the classical witchcraft we see operating in the world. Several years ago, I heard the late Rev. O.J. Phillips, then minister of The Lord's Church in Bellflower, California, tell this amazing story. A Christian man living in a nearby community called Rev. Phillips at 3 a.m. one morning. He was desperate. His wife was leaving him and was at that moment packing her bags to go. She claimed that she no longer loved him. As Rev. Phillips prayed about the situation, the Holy Spirit showed him through a vision, or word of knowledge in picture form, that a cantankerous, old sea captain living at the end of their street was releasing a spell of witchcraft on that man's wife to manipulate her. The old man was over 75 years old, had a filthy tongue, and was a heavy drinker. He was constantly leering at the man's wife whenever she was outside her house. Rev. Phillips saw that, out of the dark side of his nature, the old captain was releasing his perverted, lustful desires for the wife through foul words together with the aid of evil spirits.

Rev. Phillips explained what he was seeing to the panic-stricken husband. He asked him if there was indeed a sea captain living on his block. Amazed, the husband acknowledged that it was true. Rev. Phillips then explained how the old sea captain was using witchcraft to manipulate his wife to leave him. He began praying to bind the spell against the woman. As he broke the power of manipulation over her with the name and blood of Jesus, the man suddenly said, "Wait, my wife is unpacking. She's smiling and she just called me 'Honey.' Something's happened; whatever you're doing, keep it up 'cause its working!"

The next Sunday the couple came to church acting like radiant newlyweds, holding hands, and kissing one another. Everything went well for several months until they shared their story with another minister from a different, more conservative church. He told them they were being foolish, that there was no such thing as witchcraft in the lives of Christians, and that Rev. Phillips and The Lord's Church were in spiritual error. He even convinced them to leave The Lord's Church. They left the church feeling they had been deceived into believing that one person could influence another. However, one night several months later, Rev. Phillips received another call. It was the same distraught husband informing him that his wife had just left him... believe it or not, for the old sea captain.

In the above incident, I believe the wicked human spirit of that old man, aided by evil spirits, was lustfully reaching out to influence and control the mind and emotions of that woman. Because she was not walking in God's Spirit, she was open and susceptible to his witchcraft. Pathetically, she ended up running away with him. It is a fact that a person *can* gain influence and control over another. This is another form of witchcraft. It even happens in churches, in relationships, and in a person's own home. In this type of witchcraft, evil spirits are not always involved, but if a person persists in trying to manipulate others, evil spirits often do become involved. Many times this type of witchcraft is seen in powerful, dynamic leaders who begin to control and dominate their people. At first it may seem quite innocent, but as a leader continues to lord over others, evil spirits join in and ultimately bring great destruction. A good example of this scenario was Jim Jones. He started out as a good leader, but as he became more and more deceived, he finally reached a point where he denounced Jesus and the Bible and ultimately led almost a thousand people in mass suicide with the aid of evil spirits.

In II Corinthians 11:20, Paul warns the carnal Corinthian church,

*"For ye suffer, if a man brings you into **bondage**, if a man **devour** you, if a man takes of you, if a man exalt himself..."*

Paul is saying, "You foolish Corinthians allow carnal, worldly men to enslave you and bring you into bondage to themselves." The word "bondage," or *kata dou loo* in the Greek language, means to enslave or bring the mind and imagination under another's control. He also says that, "...if a man devour you...." The word "devour," or *katesthio*, means to take away one's property and destroy a person. Have you ever noticed how many cult leaders have their followers sell all their possessions only to take the money for themselves?

Paul is rebuking the Corinthians for allowing false apostles and leaders to control and manipulate them. A few verses earlier in II Corinthians 11:13-15, Paul explains,

Charismatic Witchcraft

*"For such are false apostles, deceitful workers, trans-
forming themselves into the apostles of Christ. And no
marvel; for satan himself is transformed into an angel of
light. Therefore it is no great thing if his ministers also be
transformed as the ministers of righteousness; whose end
shall be according to their works."*

I used to wonder how such cult leaders as Jim Jones,
Rev. Sun Moon, and Charles Manson could absolutely
control and devour their followers. How could Charles
Manson direct his underlings to murder actress Sharon
Tate and the LaBiancas when he was not even present?
How could Rev. Moon have young people out on the
streets everywhere selling flowers and trinkets and
sacrificing all they owned for the organization when he
lived in opulent luxury? How could Jim Jones lead almost
a thousand people in mass suicide? How could these cult
leaders take all the money and morals of their people and
simply use and abuse them?

God has been teaching me through His Word that men
can influence and control others through a fleshly, carnal
force called witchcraft. It is one person manipulating and
often controlling another with the evil works (influences)
of the flesh (Galatians 5:19-21).

The *almost* irresistible influence of a leader can have
very disastrous effects upon a whole nation. The Old
Testament king of Judah, Manasseh, was known as the
most evil king in the history of that nation. During the
reign of his godly father, King Hezekiah, the people had
served God, but when Manasseh became king, he set up
altars to heathen gods in the temple at Jerusalem, introduced all manner of sexual immorality, turned to familiar

spirits, astrology, and witches for direction, and even sacrificed his own children to strange gods. II Chronicles 33:9 says,

"So Manasseh made Judah and the inhabitants of Jerusalem to err, and to do worse than the heathen, whom the Lord had destroyed before the children of Israel."

Manasseh caused a whole nation to fall into terrible sin because the people became evil like their evil leader. Only by understanding the powerful effect a leader may have on his followers can cult leaders and the seemingly mindless obedience of their followers be comprehended.

Cult leaders operate in the force of witchcraft to manipulate and control their followers. Jim Jones had methodically used witchcraft on his followers and trained (actually brainwashed) them to be so obedient that they willingly took their own lives and even poisoned their own children. But Jim Jones did not start out to manipulate and control his people. According to Barbara Thielmann in her book, **The Broken God**[4], he actually began as a Methodist pastor – a good, loving, and giving man. He was heavily involved in community projects and helping the poor. But he slowly began to doubt the truth of the Bible and to idolize himself until he told his followers one day that they should go out and preach him. As he continued to exalt himself and gained more and more influence over the people, he became increasingly deluded by satan.

Jim Jones actually began to tell his friends that he himself was Jesus Christ. He began to rant against the

Bible, finally came to the place where he even threw the Bible on the ground one day, spit, and stomped on it, and screamed that too many people were looking to it instead of to him. The more he exalted himself in pride, the more his deception increased. While using trickery and fake healings and miracles to deceive, he controlled the people through fear. Finally, he abused them morally, spiritually, and physically. As Romans 1:28 says of such men,

"And even as they did not like to retain God in their knowledge, God gave them over to a reprobate mind..."

Classical witchcraft ('pharmakia' in the Greek) is defined as sorcery, or the use of drugs and spells, often accompanied by appeals to evil occult powers (demons and evil spirits), according to Webster's dictionary. But witchcraft also has another meaning – an *irresistible influence* (or manipulation). It is one person manipulating another person. It draws upon fleshly evil forces like lust, hate, envy, fear, and strife that are released out of the human heart to influence and control others. The presence of these forces can actually be sensed.

I have often been in a meeting where someone brings in a hateful, unforgiving attitude and before long the meeting is so full of strife that nothing is accomplished. Everyone leaves feeling defeated and oppressed. Years ago I used to attend a prayer meeting at a place where I worked. One of the other foremen there believed differently about certain doctrines than I did. Since there was no agreement, we made very little impact in the spiritual realm with our prayers. I could feel spiritual daggers and a heaviness coming against me. There was no liberty to pray.

All of us have witnessed that when there is a major argument between a husband and wife, a feeling of oppression enters the home. Even the dog runs and hides. The children suddenly become quiet. A chill fills the air and everyone *feels* uncomfortable. Forces of the flesh can be felt by everyone, even animals and small children.

Another area where I have frequently seen this type of control and manipulation is in dating. A young man or woman continues to date someone that they know is not good for them, someone they may not even really respect. Why? Because the forces of lust, adultery, and evil imaginations can manipulate and seduce a person.

A weeping mother called me one day years ago, to tell me that her sweet, Christian daughter was leaving home and moving into an apartment she could not even afford. This girl had stopped teaching Sunday school and had almost stopped attending church altogether. She was in rebellion against her mother. She was constantly ill. She was in danger of losing her job. Her life was a shambles.

This girl had been seeing an unsaved boyfriend almost every night, and somehow she had fallen into bondage to him. She admitted the young man was not good for her. He was constantly degrading her and cheating on her. She was compromising her Christian standards and she was breaking her family's heart.... Yet she would not or could not stop seeing him. He had an almost *irresistible influence* over her. Through the fleshly spirit of his mind, his lusts were holding this girl in bondage. II Peter 2:19 [Living Bible] explains,

"...For a man is a slave to whatever (or whoever) controls him."

The Corrupt Old Man

I have come to realize that man has a carnal, fleshly nature (the old man) which releases sinful, selfish forces through his mind. Ephesians 4:22-23 commands,

> *"That ye put off concerning the former conversation (life-style) the old man, which is corrupt according to the deceitful lusts; and be renewed in the spirit of your mind."*

You may say, "That's not me. I'm a new creature in Christ Jesus. I've put my old man to death." But all of us get angry at times; all of us occasionally feel envious of other people; all of us wrestle with evil imaginations trying to engage our thoughts. Freedom from our old man (or flesh nature) is a process, and none of us has been totally set free – yet. The Amplified Bible says it even more clearly,

> *"Strip yourselves of your former nature. – Put off and discard your old unrenewed self – which characterizes your previous manner of life and becomes corrupt through **lusts** and desires that spring from delusion; and be constantly renewed in the spirit of your mind – having a fresh mental and spiritual attitude; and put on the new nature (the regenerated self) created in God's image (Godlike) in true righteousness and holiness."*

We are commanded to put off and strip ourselves of the carnal, fleshly spirit of our mind because it is through the mind or soul that the works and forces of the flesh are released. Witchcraft, that manipulating influence over others, is one of those works of the flesh that operates out of the carnal (soulish) man. Galatians 5:19-21 says,

> *"Now the works of the flesh are manifest, which are these, adultery, fornication, uncleanness, lasciviousness, idolatry, **witchcraft**, hatred, variance, emulations, wrath, strife, seditions, heresies, envyings, murders, drunkenness, revelings, and such like..."*

But you still may say that you do not do those things. The Living Bible paraphrases some of these words as impure thoughts, jealousy, anger, criticisms, selfishness... and witchcraft. If you will be honest with yourself, you will admit that these forces sometimes do work in your life. The Bible warns us about these things so we can recognize them in their infancy and deal with them before they become major strongholds that can defeat us.

Spoken Thunderbolts

Just as anger and selfishness often manifest in our lives, we must be aware that we can also fall into the controlling and manipulating of others – or witchcraft. We do not mean to control others, but we do, in fact, often try to assert our own wills over those of others. We must be careful that all of our actions, words, and deeds are released out of our reborn, recreated, God-joined spirits and not out of the fleshly, carnal thoughts of our minds that are not yet completely renewed to the mind of Christ. The unrenewed human spirit and carnal mind operate in

satan's domain while our godly reborn spirit draws its life
and power from the Holy Spirit of God. In Matthew
15:19, Jesus said,

> *"For out of the heart (soulish realm) proceed evil
> thoughts, murders, adulteries, fornications, thefts, false wit-
> ness, blasphemies..."*

These evil deeds begin as thoughts that are most often
released from the mind, will, and emotions by the *words*
of our mouths. Speaking of our words, Jesus said in
Matthew 15:18,

> *"But those things which proceed out of the mouth come
> forth from the heart; and they defile the man."*

This means a man's words will tell you what is in his
heart, whether good or evil. Matthew 12:34-35 says,

> *"... for out of the abundance of the heart, the mouth
> speaketh. A good man out of the good treasure of the heart
> bringeth forth good things: and an evil man out of the evil
> treasure bringeth forth evil things."*

Because our words reveal the motivations of our hearts,
we will be judged by our words, according to Jesus in
Matthew 12:37,

> *"For by thy words thou shalt be justified and by thy words
> thou shalt be condemned."*

Words are extremely powerful. God used words to create the whole earth, and He has given us that same creative ability with our words. We can either bless people or we can curse them by what we say. Our words should bring healing, deliverance, salvation, and prosperity to people's lives if we are filled with the Spirit of God. Too many times our critical and judgmental words have the characteristics of satan who steals, kills, and destroys.

Carnal men in positions of authority can actually manipulate and control others; they can use their powerful words to damage and destroy the lives of others. Luke 9:51-56 gives us a vivid description of the disciples being tempted to misuse their authority until Jesus showed them their error.

> *"And it came to pass, when the time was come that He should be received up, He steadfastly set His face to go to Jerusalem, and sent messengers before His face: and they went, and entered into a village of the Samaritans, to make ready for Him. And they did not receive Him, because His face was as though He would go to Jerusalem. And when His disciples James and John saw this, they said, Lord, wilt Thou that we command fire to come down from heaven, and consume them, even as Elijah did? But He turned, and rebuked them, and said, Ye know not what manner of spirit ye are of. For the Son of man is not come to destroy men's lives, but to save them. And they went to another village."*

James and John became angry at the Samaritans. They wanted to command down fire to destroy the Samaritans withstanding Jesus. But James and John were speaking out of the flesh and the carnal thinking of their old natures.

Jesus said to them, "You do not know what *spirit* you are of." Jesus rebuked them because they did not realize they were in the flesh (the spirit of their minds) and not inspired by the Spirit of God. The Spirit of God is grace, mercy, and love. Jesus came to save, heal, deliver, and set men free – not to destroy their lives.

Prayer or Prey

While we are discussing the power of words, one of the ways that one person may be manipulating and controlling another is through selfish, soulish prayers. That person uses his prayers to attempt to bear pressure upon the mind, will, and emotions (or soul) of another person to achieve his own desires.

I have seen this kind of manipulation at work over and over in the realm of dating and potential marriage partners. For example, a young man may desire to court a certain young lady. Because he feels so strongly and passionately about her, he assumes that she is God's choice for his mate. Even though he prays and asks the Lord about her, his prayers are really just a plea for confirmation of his own desires because his mind is already made up. He may even use scriptures out of context, like Mark 11:24, which says, "What things soever ye desire, when ye pray, *believe* that ye receive them, and ye shall have them," to mean that he can pray and claim her by faith as his bride. In his imagination, she is already his wife. To make matters worse, deceiving spirits can then set up circumstances that appear to be the desired confirmation and answer to prayer. He may even be fully convinced that he has heard directly from the Lord that she is to be his wife.

As circumstances continue to encourage him, he begins to pray that the young lady's eyes be opened to receive the same "revelation" of their "preordained marriage." In his heart he has put a claim on her and with his prayers he is attempting to place a form of spiritual bondage on her soul that will enslave her to him. In some instances, while unaware of what is happening in the spiritual and soulish realm, the young lady may feel drawn to the young man and find herself constantly thinking about him even though she is not attracted to him in the natural. The soul of the young man is actually reaching out to the soul of the young woman to form a soul tie and enslave her to him.

As a single pastor, I have often been the target of soulish prayers and manipulations. Many young (and some not so young) women have been convinced that I was to be their husband. They have come to me with numerous "confirmations" that they honestly believe the Lord has given them. One young woman had over seventy supposed confirmations that I was to marry her, and yet the Lord had never spoken to me concerning her. (When it comes to marriage, God always speaks to both parties.) Because these women had asserted their own wills and desires over the will of God, they had opened themselves to a spirit of deception that was actually playing games with their wills and emotions. Having become deceived, they were unaware that their prayers had become a form of charismatic witchcraft.

Manipulating Word Curses

Our spirits are powerful, more powerful than we often realize. We can bless and deliver people through the Holy Spirit or curse them through our carnal, fleshly human spirits. When we speak evil of another person, we may be cursing them. Galatians 5:15 warns,

> *"But if ye bite and devour one another, take heed that ye are not consumed one of another."*

Also, James 3:8-9 cautions,

> *"But the tongue can no man tame; it is an unruly evil, full of deadly poison. Therewith bless we God, even the Father; and therewith curse we men, which are made after the similitude of God."*

Our words can be so spiritually powerful that they can curse and devour the lives of others.

I once heard a minister relate this interesting example of how a well-meaning, but misguided individual could use soulish, manipulating words against others. At a prayer meeting one night, this minister was walking around the altar where several members of the church were earnestly praying. As he walked by one of the most faithful women in his congregation, he stopped. He was horrified to hear her praying very powerfully, "God, I bind Brother Dyer; I bind him to go broke; I bind Brother and Sister Dyer to lose everything so they'll have to close down their business! God, what I bind on earth is bound in heaven!" The sad part was that the Dyer's business was *indeed* on the verge of bankruptcy.

When the puzzled minister asked the woman why she was praying that way, the woman replied that the Dyers had once attended the prayer meetings and been active in the church. But now their business was taking all their time and efforts and they were no longer able to come to all the church services and activities. The minister sadly asked her, "Did it ever occur to you to ask God to bless their business so they could hire extra help? If they had extra help, they could take care of the business and still attend the services!"

Our prayers should always be directed to blessing people, not cursing them. Even though that woman had been used mightily by God in the church to prophesy and minister to others, she was now misusing her authority as a believer to manipulate and curse the Dyers. She was very sincere and loved the church and the Dyers, and yet she was ignorantly using charismatic witchcraft against them. When shown her error, however, the woman was very apologetic and repentant.

What grieves me so much is that I have seen this misuse of spiritual power or witchcraft in so many of our charismatic churches. A minister I spoke with recently said that he had gone to take over a new pastorate. He had immediately established with the elders that *he* was the anointed leader that God had sent them. The church was no longer to be governed by a board of directors or a group of elders, although they could serve in an advisory capacity and help in the decision making process. As he began to preach and teach in that church, people started attending from the community and soon the church had doubled in size. People were being saved, healed, and delivered.

Unfortunately, a part of the church board became very upset; they did not want the church to grow. They did not like people from the outside coming to their services, especially those who were unclean, had a different life-style, or did not live according to their personal standards. They liked their little church family the way it was and wanted no outsiders. Soon those unhappy board members began speaking against the pastor and his wife. Their little faction caused strife and mistrust to come into the church and destroy the move of God. They were guilty of falling into witchcraft, gossip, and word curses against the pastor and the work of God in that church!

A person may become involved in witchcraft or manipulation quite innocently. He or she may think the pastor or someone in authority is not doing a good job or that they are even out of God's will. He may begin to pray his own will into a situation and not ask that God's will be done. At the same time, he may subtly undermine the person in authority to others, suggesting they may not be doing a good job. This is very dangerous. It is witchcraft and rebellion against authority!

False Prophets

Even though I believe in prophecy and have met true prophets, I have seen another manifestation of charismatic witchcraft in false prophecies and false prophets. I have witnessed many self-proclaimed prophets in churches and Christian circles prophesying out of their own carnal human spirits (minds) and desires, rather than by the Spirit of God. They are actually influencing many Christians and causing them to go astray. Jeremiah 23 speaks of these false prophets in the house of God. Verse 11 says,

"For both prophet and priest are profane; yea, in My house have I found their wickedness, saith the Lord."

I recently had an experience that illustrates how these self-proclaimed prophets may use their words to try to manipulate others. A man calling himself a prophet came to my office one day, insisting he had a word from God for me that I needed to hear at once. Since he did not have an appointment and I had a full schedule, I could not see him that day. I knew this man and his ministry. I did not actually believe he was a prophet, but I had compassion for him as a hurting human being who was living in his car. I also knew he desperately needed finances. I instructed my secretary to schedule an appointment with him for the following week and to have a check ready for him. When she talked to him, he became angry and refused the appointment. He insisted that God said I should see him immediately or not at all. Using the phrase, "the Lord says," he attempted to manipulate us into an immediate appointment.

I happened to come across him on the street the next day, and he stressed to me that I had missed God by not listening to him when he came to my office. He also told me that he had refused the appointment. I quietly informed him that since he had cancelled his appointment,

I had cancelled the check I had planned to give him. The next day he tried in vain to set up another appointment....

Jesus said in Matthew 24:24, that in the last days there would arise false Christs and false prophets, and II Peter 2:1 tells us they will be among us. In other words, they will be in our churches. He warned us that many who claim to represent God would be lost. Matthew 7:21-23 says,

> *"Not every one that saith to Me, Lord, Lord, shall enter the kingdom of heaven; but he that doeth the will of My Father which is in heaven. Many will say to Me in that day, Lord, Lord, have we not **prophesied** in Thy name?... And I will then profess unto them, I never knew you: depart from Me, ye that work iniquity."*

Many false prophets began as true prophets of God. But as they compromised the Word of God and began relying on their own personal charisma instead of the Holy Spirit to minister, they started manipulating people with their words. As they became more and more deceived, they eventually prophesied their own desires and made merchandise of the gift of God. The Lord's punishment will fall on these false prophets. He will not allow men to defile His gifts and His holy name; He will severely judge those who misrepresent Him.

A respected pastor shared how a well known evangelist and prophet noticed an attractive young girl in the audience of an evangelistic rally one night. As lust arose in his heart, he prophesied to her. He was many years older than the girl and was prophesying to her out of his own carnal human spirit. He said to her, "I see our two spirits like doves flying up into the heights and joining together to spread this glorious gospel." As the evangelist prophesied to her in this way, his carnal human spirit reached out to control her. This is charismatic witchcraft – forbidden by God. Sadly, the gullible young girl believed him and eventually married him, but soon after, they separated. Needless to say, their marriage was a total disaster, and the evangelist lost his ministry.

Christians have to be on guard and judge by the Holy Spirit the prophecies they receive, especially those containing personal, specific direction for their lives. I believe that *true* prophets can give directional words, but I am apprehensive and guarded about prophecies that tell a person who to marry, where he should move, or what sex his children will be. I have heard many grandiose prophecies predicting worldwide ministries for individuals that have little interest in ministry. We must beware of prophetic words that puff up individuals to make them vain. Jeremiah 3:16 warns,

> *"Thus saith the Lord of Hosts, hearken not unto the words of the prophets that prophesy unto you: they make you vain: they speak a vision of their **own** heart, and not out of the mouth of the Lord."*

Revelation 19:10 tells us "that the testimony of Jesus is the spirit of prophecy." All prophecy should bring glory to Jesus! (An excellent book giving guidelines to personal prophecy is the book by Dr. Bill Hamon, **Prophets And Personal Prophecy,** Destiny Image Publications, Shippensburg, PA, 1987.)

Charismatic Witchcraft

In the area of personal prophecy, there are many dangers. Many years ago a young, single evangelist, Brant Baker, had a powerful healing ministry in Long Beach, California. I was attending a home Bible study at the time and many of us would go together to Brant Baker's meetings. We were all young and inexperienced in the spiritual gifts and were fascinated by the healings and manifestations of the Holy Spirit in those meetings. Two of the newly saved young girls from my study fell into a common trap of satan. One of the girls became infatuated with Brant and began to idolize him. The other girl, watching her friend care so deeply for him, told her one day that she had dreamed that her friend would marry Brant before Christmas. As a sign from God, she gave her friend a personal prophecy that as she sat in the second row of the auditorium, Brant's eyes would catch her eyes.

The girls continued to attend the meetings, and eventually managed to sit in the second row. As Brant preached that night, he glanced around the room and his eyes happened to fall upon the girl. She took this as a confirmation that they would indeed be married. Christmas came and went, and Brant never even once approached the girl. Devastated, she turned against her friend in anger for giving her that false word. She also left the Bible study and the Lord, feeling that God had lied to her and let her down. Finally, she moved in with an unsaved boyfriend and became pregnant... all because of a false word. I learned through this sad experience to carefully judge all personal prophecies and to protect those God had put in my charge.

SEDUCTIONS EXPOSED

Speaking of self-appointed prophets, God warns the people not to listen to them because they only speak words that people want to hear, not what God is truly saying. Ezekiel 13:6 states,

"They have seen vanity and lying divination, saying, the Lord saith: and the Lord hath not sent them: and they have made others to hope that they would confirm the word."

There are many Christians who follow supposed prophets around hoping to receive a word from the Lord. People who are constantly seeking prophetic words from those supposed prophets can actually fall into divination and fortune-telling and become subject to guidance from evil spirits. There is a time and a season to look to the prophet for direction, but all Christians must learn to hear from the Lord directly for themselves. In any case, *most often* prophets only confirm what the Lord has already spoken to the heart of the individual.

We must renew our minds to the Word of God so we can test and prove all prophetic words by the written Word. Paul emphasizes in I Thessalonians 5:20-21, that we must have the proper attitude concerning prophecy. He says,

"Despise not prophesyings. Prove all things; hold fast that which is good."

Every true prophetic word must be in line with Bible scriptures. Any revelations that contradict or add to the Bible must be rejected.

True and accurate prophecy is a beautiful and precious gift from God. It is a word in due season that exhorts, edifies, and encourages. It brings hope and faith into the individual and builds the body of Christ. It will often enable a person to endure very difficult and trying circumstances while building faith and patience in that person's life. In II Chronicles 20:20b, God promises,

*"Believe the Lord God and so shall ye be established; believe **His** prophets, so ye shall prosper."*

Our carnal minds are often unable to discern what is of God and what has come from the heart of a man. As we allow the Word of God to transform and renew our minds, we are more able to prove what is of God, what is of man, and what is from satan. Romans 12:2 says,

*"And be not conformed to this world; but be ye transformed by the renewing of your mind, that ye may **prove** what is that good, and acceptable, and perfect will of God."*

Scriptural Manipulation

Lately, I have seen Spirit-filled Christians who cloak their selfish, carnal desires under spiritual pretense. They desire to do something for God but they want to do it immediately without allowing God to prepare them. They are often unhappy with their spiritual position in life so they begin to prophesy out of their soulish desires trying to convince others it is God speaking.

For instance, I was told of a woman and her daughter who were praying in tongues while supposedly writing down messages from God. I suspect this was actually automatic handwriting, an occultic practice where evil spirits cause the hand to write or draw a message from demons. One of the supposed messages from God was that the daughter was to leave and divorce her husband so she would be free to travel and minister worldwide. She felt that she was called as a teacher and had been desiring a traveling ministry. She also considered her husband to be a hindrance to the fulfillment of her calling since he had no desire to travel and was not even in support of her ministry. The written message was absolutely not the Spirit of God speaking. God does *not* contradict His Word.... He hates divorce.

Paul warned about those who would try to change the gospel for their own purposes in Galatians 1:9,

> *"... if any man preach any other gospel unto you than that ye have received, let him be accursed ('anathema' – under divine curse)."*

Paul wrote to the foolish Galatians who were being deceived by this form of influence and witchcraft, asking them in Galatians 3:1,3,

> *"O foolish Galatians, who hath **bewitched** you, that ye should not obey the truth, before whose eyes Jesus Christ has been evidently set forth, crucified among you... Are ye so foolish? Having begun in the Spirit, are ye now made perfect by the flesh?"*

From the earliest days of the church, satan has tried to destroy the simple truth of the gospel by distorting and adding the bondages of tradition to the doctrine of Christ just as we see happening in every cult. The early church in Jerusalem had a sect arise in their leadership which taught, according to Acts 15:1, "Except ye (the Gentiles) be circumcised after the manner of Moses, ye cannot be saved." They were trying to take away the liberty of Jesus Christ and replace it with the bondage of the law. They were actually using the law to manipulate the newly converted Gentiles to follow man's rules of acceptance. Peter addressed them in Acts 15:9-11, saying,

> *"And (we must) put no difference between us (Jews) and them (Gentiles), purifying their hearts by faith. Now therefore why tempt ye God, to put a yoke upon the neck of the disciples, which neither our fathers nor we were able to bear? But we believe that through the grace of the Lord Jesus Christ we shall be saved, even as they."*

Several years ago, a close friend of mine became involved with a group called the "Children of God." He had been wounded by some of his friends in a traditional Christian church and would often come to me and tell me how loving and Christ-like the "Children of God" were. He gradually became fully indoctrinated into that cult's practices, as taught by their leader, Moses David, in his "Mo Letters." I was totally dismayed one day when I learned of one of the doctrines of the cult called the "flirty fish policy." According to this policy, the young women in the cult were encouraged to visit bars and nightclubs where they were instructed to "pick up" young men and have sexual relations with them. By having the women seduce the young men and telling them about Jesus, they hoped to attract new cult members.

When I asked my friend how he could possibly justify such a practice in light of all the scripture against fornication, he quietly replied that Paul told us, in I Corinthians 9:22, we were to be all things to all men that we might win some. I was saddened and frustrated to see that my friend was under such manipulation and control by the cult leaders that he could no longer judge such practices by scripture for himself. He accepted without question whatever the leaders told him. I tried in vain to show him that he had believed another gospel... not the gospel of Jesus Christ.

The Jezebel Spirit

Another area where witchcraft is often seen is in the woman who asserts authority over men and tries to control them. God, throughout the Bible, forbids women to control men or to usurp their authority. In Genesis 3:16, God told Eve,

> *"... and thy desire shall be to thy husband, and he shall rule over thee."*

In the divine order established by God for the marriage relationship, men and women are to submit (or adapt) to one another, but the man is given headship. In Ephesians 5:21-25, Paul clearly explains,

Charismatic Witchcraft

"Submitting yourselves one to another in the fear of God. Wives submit yourselves unto your own husbands, as unto the Lord. For the husband is the head of the wife, even as Christ is the head of the church: and He is the saviour of the body. Therefore as the church is subject unto Christ, so let the wives be to their own husbands in every thing. Husbands, love your wives, even as Christ also loved the church, and gave Himself for it."

In the Old Testament, King Ahab lost his kingdom because of his overpowering wife, Jezebel. Instead of righteously ruling the kingdom God had given him, he allowed his heathen wife, Jezebel, to reign over the land. She brought all kinds of abominations into the nation, including Baal (or satan) worship and caused not only her husband, Ahab, to sin but also perverted the whole nation. I Kings 21:25 [Living Bible] says,

"No one else was so completely sold out to the devil as Ahab, for his wife encouraged (incited or manipulated) him to do every sort of evil."

That Jezebel spirit of witchcraft still tries to influence the end-time church of Thyatira which is one of the types of churches that exist today. God says in Revelation 2:20-21,

"Notwithstanding I have a few things against thee, because thou sufferest that woman Jezebel, which calleth herself a prophetess, to teach and to seduce My servants to commit fornication, and to eat things sacrificed to idols. And I gave her space to repent of her fornication; and she repented not."

- 129 -

I believe the Jezebel spirit is in operation whenever a person of lower authority tries to manipulate or control a person of higher authority over them. It is seen in wives that try to control their husbands, but it also operates in churches and other organizations, and it is not limited to women. In other words, men can also operate under a Jezebel spirit of witchcraft.

We have seen people with this spirit of manipulation many times at the Eagle's Nest Christian Fellowship. Some time ago we saw it operate through an individual who wanted to participate in the church decision-making process without going through the period of servanthood and discipleship we require of all those raised up to positions of authority. He promised large donations to our ministry, frequently maneuvered himself to be around the guest speakers, and continually offered his advice on church matters. He repeatedly promoted himself and always seemed to have a "word from God" for me and my guest speakers. One night I prevented him from mingling with our guest speakers after a service. Angered and offended, he actually left the church. His commitment to the church was only as strong as his ability to influence and rub shoulders with the leaders.

Walking in the Safety Zone

You may ask, "How does witchcraft touch a Christian? Can a Christian really be affected by someone trying to manipulate him with their prayers or by giving him a false prophetic word? Aren't we automatically protected by the blood of Jesus?" I recently received a letter from a girl who wrote, "Pastor Gary, I have tried to manipulate you long enough with my prayers. I want you to know that I am giving up because nothing is working out. You won't do what I want so I am giving up on you." I do not know what she wanted of me, but I do know that if enough people are praying for me to do something, it may affect me if I am not walking very strongly in the Spirit. Here is the key. If you are not walking in the Spirit and are living according to the flesh and its carnal desires, other people who are also in the flesh may manipulate and control you.

Witchcraft can operate whenever the carnal human nature with its fleshly works of one person reaches out to influence and manipulate another person. The only way to overcome the influence of witchcraft is to walk in the Spirit and develop the fruits of the Holy Spirit. But to be honest, none of us stays in the Spirit at all times. A person may be walking in the Spirit, but he begins to watch a television program full of lust, divorce, hatred, and violence and suddenly he is gratifying and reinforcing his flesh nature. For instance, a wife may become angry and embittered with her husband, and suddenly she is walking according to the flesh and its passions. When a person moves out of walking in the Spirit, he is vulnerable to manipulation and control by the lustful passions of others. Instead of being able to respond to an angry accusation with kindness and gentleness, he may be pulled into a heated argument.

For example, a Spirit-filled wife may be married to an unsaved and unruly man. She may love the Lord with all her heart and be involved in church. She may be praying for his salvation and spending her days in prayer, thanking and praising God for saving her husband... until the soap opera comes on the television at two o'clock every day. Then she *has* to see what is happening to her favorite characters and imaginary friends even though the program is full of deceit, unfaithfulness and adultery, divorce, incest, homosexuality, etc. Because she is filling herself with the lusts of the flesh, she is no longer able to maintain her walk in the Spirit. When her husband comes home angry because dinner is not ready and on the table waiting for him, she snaps back at him, and soon they are in a major argument.

If the wife had stayed in the Spirit and filled her mind with the Word of God rather than the soap opera on television, she would have been able to react lovingly to his anger, soothing his temper without allowing his anger to manipulate her into an argument. It is hard for a person to stay cruel and abrasive toward someone who is being loving and kind to them. As Proverbs 15:1 says,

> *"A soft answer turneth away wrath: but grievous words stir up anger."*

Again, the only way to resist the influence of witchcraft is to walk in the Spirit and develop the fruits of the Spirit. Galatians 5:16 says,

> *"... walk in the spirit, and ye shall **not** fulfill the lust of the flesh."*

Charismatic Witchcraft

Witchcraft will not work against a Christian who is walking in the Spirit and who has died to the lusts of his carnal nature. Sadly though, many Christians do not feed on the Word of God daily or maintain the prayer life necessary to stay in the Spirit. They do not go to church where they are refreshed and built up in their inner man. They do not fellowship with other Christians. Because we become like those with whom we associate, it is only when we spend time with God that we will demonstrate His character and the fruits of His Holy Spirit!

To walk in the Spirit means to allow the Holy Spirit to control every aspect of our lives. Galatians 5:22-25 [Living Bible] tells us,

> *"But when the Holy Spirit **controls** our lives He will produce this kind of fruit in us: love, joy, peace, patience, kindness, goodness, faithfulness, gentleness, and self-control... Those who belong to Christ have nailed their evil desires to His cross and crucified them there. If we are living now by the Holy Spirit's power, let us follow the Holy Spirit's leading in every part of our lives."*

There are times when a person may have good, and even godly intentions, but he is still operating in the flesh. Several years ago a couple in our church had a daughter involved with Mormonism. They tried to tell her it was a cult and that she was serving the wrong Jesus. They bombarded her with scripture and continually confronted her. I suggested to them that instead of trying to argue and convince her, they should show her the fruits of the Spirit. By demonstrating love and patience toward her, they would make Jesus more real to her. Following my suggestion, they continued to pray for her and to love her, and the power of Jesus eventually overcame her resistance. About a month later, she came to her parents and said, "I want this Jesus that you serve because mine doesn't do anything for me!" She was won to the Lord through the fruits of the Spirit, not through argument or strife.

Abused And Misused Gifts

We are told, in Romans 11:29, that the gifts and callings of God are without repentance. One of the meanings of this verse is that once God gives His gifts to a man, He does not repent and remove them when the man sins or errs. Because of this, Christians who do not crucify the flesh nature may fall back into old carnal patterns of living and still be demonstrating spiritual gifts and power. The sad fact is that some Christians even fall into using their gifts for their own benefit and financial gain. This selfish misuse is a form of charismatic witchcraft which bears evil fruits instead of those that glorify Jesus.

I am convinced by scripture that a person can illegally operate in spiritual power (even in the name of Jesus) and yet be rejected by God. Matthew 7:20-23 warns,

> *"Wherefore by their **fruits** ye shall know them (not their gifts!). Not every one that saith unto Me, Lord, Lord, shall enter into the kingdom of heaven; but he that doeth the will of My Father which is in heaven. Many will say to Me in that day, Lord, Lord, have we not prophesied in Thy name? and in Thy name have cast out devils? and in Thy name done many*

Charismatic Witchcraft

wonderful works? And then I will profess unto them, I never knew you: depart from Me, ye that work iniquity."

The word iniquity means lawlessness. Many Christians unlawfully use God's gifts and His power to satisfy their carnal desires. For example, a person may prophesy, not by the Spirit of God, but out of his own heart. He may manipulate people prophetically for his own gain or attempt to control a church to satisfy his own selfish desires. I have seen insecure pastors who control their people by false prophecies threatening them that if they leave the church they will lose their salvation. I have been grieved by ministers who promise healing and deliverance to those who will give the largest offerings. Intimidation, selfishness, and greed are not fruits of God's Spirit. Jesus is saying that we are to look at the fruits of a man's life, not the gifts in which he operates, to see whether his ministry is of God.

A classic example of a minister with powerful gifts, but poor fruit, would be the young evangelist we had minister one evening at the Eagle's Nest. He moved in a mighty word of knowledge, he discerned the oppression of evil spirits in people's lives, and when he prayed for people or even breathed on them, they fell under God's power. During his awesome ministry, people lined up at the altar to give testimonies of the miraculous healing and deliverance they had just received. I was away on a crusade of my own on that particular evening and had left my associate pastors in charge of the services. Taking advantage of my absence, that young minister, using his tremendous charisma and anointing, decided to take a special offering for one of his own projects and launched into a twenty minute "push" for sacrificial giving from our people. Because he had not previously alerted my pastors that he would take a special second offering, they were completely taken off-guard. By telling the people the money was for Bibles and evangelistic materials for overseas, he raised fifty five hundred dollars.

My staff became extremely alarmed the next day when he came to our office demanding the money immediately because his wife had to pay some bills at home. We learned later from an associate of his that none of the money had been used for Bibles or materials overseas. The pastors and I agreed that he had manipulated the people with his gifts and mighty ministry to give him a large offering which he subsequently used only for selfish gain. Later, word also came to us that while ministering at another church, he had taken a young girl back to his hotel room and fallen in adultery with her.

As his character flaws and poor fruits manifested in more and more churches all across the nation, doors of ministry closed to him. He had great gifts that God gives without repentance, but he had abused and misused them, and sadly, many saints were stumbled in the process. Jesus warned us of such men when He said, in Matthew 15:15,

> *"Beware of false prophets which come to you in sheep's clothing but inwardly they are ravening wolves."*

The manipulations of this young evangelist occurred in several areas. He deceived the pastors by not alerting them to the special offering. He lied when he told the people that the money would go for Bibles overseas, and he even used his spirituality to gain sexual favors from a young girl.

Spiritual Immunity

How then can we protect ourselves from those who use charismatic witchcraft and carnal manipulation against us? I want to share three ways to defeat the force of witchcraft. *First*, make a firm decision to live a Spirit-controlled life that has put to death the works of the flesh. Romans 8:5-6 clearly says,

> *"For they that are after the flesh do mind the things of the flesh; but they that are after the Spirit, the things of the Spirit. For to be carnally minded is death; but to be spiritually minded is life and peace."*

Carefully examine your own heart and motivations and repent and ask forgiveness of any witchcraft, manipulation and unlawful control you have exerted over others. What you do unto others *will* eventually be done to you. In Galatians 6:7-8, God warns,

> *"Be not deceived; God is not mocked: for whatsoever a man soweth, that shall he also reap. For he that soweth to his flesh shall of the flesh reap corruption, but he that soweth to the Spirit shall of the Spirit reap life everlasting."*

Secondly, stand firmly on God's promise that witchcraft has no power against you when you are in Christ and He is in you. I John 4:4 [AMP] assures us,

"Little children ye are of God – you belong to Him – and have [already] defeated and overcome them [the agents of antichrist] because He who lives in you is greater (mightier) than he who is in the world."

In Jesus, your spirit is more powerful than the spirit of witchcraft. Claim your inheritance as a child of God. Isaiah 54:17 promises that,

"No weapon that is formed against thee shall prosper; and every tongue that shall rise against thee in judgment thou shalt condemn. This is the heritage of the servants of the Lord, and their righteousness is of Me, saith the Lord."

Finally, resist the forces (works) of the flesh with the forces (fruits) of the Spirit (the Spirit of Christ). Romans 8:2 says,

"For the law of the Spirit of life in Christ Jesus hath made me free from the law of sin and death."

All the works of the flesh are under the law of sin and death, but the law of the Spirit of life in Jesus has made us free from these works of the flesh. The Holy Spirit enables us to resist wrath and anger with meekness, to resist strife with peace and joy, to resist lust with purity and holiness, to resist hatred with love and forgiveness, to resist drunkenness with temperance and self-control.... We can resist any carnal spirit under the law of sin and death with the Spirit of Christ, because against such, according to Galatians 5:23, "there is no law."

If others persecute, curse or do evil to you, bless them. Romans 12:14 admonishes,

"Bless them which persecute you: bless, and curse not."

Do not fight on their level because you will lose spiritually. Fight on the level of Christ Jesus and God will win. Do not bind the person or curse them or even wish evil against them. Bless them! Make I Corinthians 4:12 your testimony, "Being reviled, we bless...." It will be difficult for your enemies to continue to do evil against you when you are blessing them and showing them the love of Christ.

Rescue from Spiritual Bondage

If you see someone in spiritual bondage to another person, you can use the spiritual weapons Jesus has given us to set that person free. One of those weapons is binding and loosing. According to Matthew 18:18,

"Verily I say unto you, whatsoever you shall bind on earth shall be bound in heaven; and whatsoever ye shall loose on earth shall be loosed in heaven."

You, as a Christian, have God's legal permission to bind any evil, tormenting spirits and to loose their captives from any bondages. God has given you spiritual weapons such as the Word, the blood of Jesus, the name of Jesus, overcoming faith, and your spoken words of authority to pull down satan's strongholds in people's lives. Paul says of these powerful weapons, in II Corinthians 10:4-5,

SEDUCTIONS EXPOSED

"For the weapons of our warfare are not carnal, but mighty through God to the pulling down of strongholds; casting down imaginations, and every high thing that exalteth itself against the knowledge of God, and bringing into captivity every thought to the obedience of Christ."

In the earlier case of the young Christian girl who was in bondage to the worldly, unsaved boyfriend, I prayed with her mother and together we bound the spirit of lust, according Matthew 18:18, and asked God to open her eyes and break the bondage she was under to that young man. We loosed that girl from the young man's evil imaginations and fleshly holds on her by the power of Jesus' name. We cancelled every evil assignment against her and asked God to restore her love for her family and the church. I also told her mother to resist her daughter's rebellion and strife with love and patience and not to fight or quarrel with her but instead to show her God's love. We both felt confident that God had heard our prayers and was already intervening in the girl's life.

About two weeks later, I received a phone call from her excited and happy mother. The girl had suddenly seen the young man's true nature and had become repulsed by his advances and left him. She had moved home again, had started attending church and teaching Sunday school, and her health had returned. The forces of the Spirit of Christ in that mother overcame the powers of darkness working in the daughter.... Love and faith are always victorious!

If you have a family member or loved one who is in bondage to someone or is being manipulated, I am going to show you how to pray for that person and loose them from that influence. We are going to bind the strong man and loose the captive. As we agree together in prayer, God will hear us and answer our prayer. According to Matthew 18:19, Jesus promises,

"Again I (Jesus) say to you, that if two of you agree on earth as touching anything that they shall ask, it shall be done for them of My Father which is in heaven."

Pray with me this way, "Father, I exalt and praise you that nothing is too hard for you. I thank you that even though my loved one is being manipulated or controlled or being prophetically misled, you have given us the greater power to set them free. You have given us the name of Jesus, the blood of Jesus, the weapons of our warfare which are mighty through Jesus for the pulling down of strongholds and every high thing that exalts itself against the name of Jesus.

"We lift up that loved one to you, Father, and we ask you to break every soulish power that is working against them, every spirit of witchcraft that has been deceiving them, every carnal manipulation that has been drawing them into bondage to lust, strife, hatred, or any other works of the flesh. We bind the evil spirits working against them, and we break their strongholds over that person in the mighty name of Jesus. We cast them down *now*.

"We thank you now, Father, that as we see the walls of bondage tumbling down, we ask the Holy Spirit to convict our loved ones of sin, of righteousness, and of judgment. We ask the Holy Spirit to draw them back to Jesus, to cause them to seek out righteousness. We thank you,

Lord, that their hunger for Christian fellowship is growing right now. We thank you for holy angels that are around them and protecting them. We thank you for the blood of Jesus upon their minds to protect them from any more influence from these outside forces. We put the blood of Jesus upon them now, and we claim in Jesus' name that they will not be wrongfully influenced or controlled by any person or thing. We thank you, Father, that we are going to see their salvation, their restoration, and their complete freedom in Jesus' mighty name. Amen!!!"

ABOMINABLE OCCULTIC OBJECTS AND PRACTICES

Forbidden Practices

Has it ever occurred to you that certain innocent statues, pictures, and household ornaments can actually be habitations for evil spirits? Or, that good luck charms, amulets, and assorted jewelry from certain cultures can actually invite demonic oppression and curses on your life? Have you ever seen households where everything that can possibly go wrong seems to? Do you know people who seem to experience disaster after disaster? Their children are always in trouble, there is a constant battle with sickness in the home, they are anxiety ridden and full of emotional turmoil, there is never enough money to pay all the bills, and they can never hold down a job. Some people actually seem doomed to failure.... Have you ever wondered why? We have seen that there can be a transference of spirits from those we associate with and also from the world system. But I want to show you further that a person can also open a disastrous door to demonic influence and oppression by dabbling in the occult and even by possessing objects that have occultic implications. It is my belief that in many cases even the transference of wrong spirits, ungodly soul ties, and the manipulation of witchcraft can be initiated and reinforced by the occultic objects and practices we will discuss in this chapter.

Rachel, one of the girls that works at the Eagle's Nest, recently shared her startling testimony with me. At a gathering one holiday, the family decided to play with a Ouija board as a diversion. Being an unbeliever in the supernatural, Rachel actually defied the board and dared it to talk to her. The board spelled out that it had "no business" with her, but the experience did have very drastic and terrible consequences for the next ten years of her life. A short time later as she sat watching a horror movie on television, an overwhelming fear came upon her. It was as if a black cloud had entered the room and enveloped her. For the next year, Rachel was literally immobilized by fear and depression. Until that time, she had led a normal life, but now she had become a manic depressive overnight.

During the next few years, Rachel struggled with depression and fear, and even attempted suicide many times. She tried to kill her husband on two occasions and would often go into violent fits of rage. Once she chased her children around the house with a butcher knife, and they soon learned to duck as she threw household items at them. Although Rachel was searching for reality, she was looking in all the wrong places. First, she played with horoscopes; then she went to a tea leaf reader. From there she visited a spiritualist, and finally both she and her husband and also her children became involved with transcendental meditation and mind science religions. She was actually drawn to the occult and tried every method it could offer to find relief from the tormenting depression that controlled her life. Even as she delved deeper and deeper into occultic practices, she found only increasing torment and fear. Instead of the freedom she sought, she sank into bondage to drugs and alcohol.

During the time Rachel was dabbling in occultic practices, she was secretly watching Christian television when no one else was home. One day she accepted Jesus into her life in response to the invitation given during a Christian program. For the first time in her life, joy began to flood into her soul. Three Spirit-filled cousins who had been praying for her salvation for seventeen years explained to Rachel that she had to renounce all occultic involvement and confess it as sin. As she did so, the horrible depression that had held her captive immediately left and peace filled her mind. God healed her, set her free, and gave her a new life with purpose and fulfillment she had never known before!

Not only are worldly people involved in the occult, but many Christians are ignorantly held captive to disease, poverty, and failure because of their abominable ignorance of God's Word. Isaiah 5:13 declares,

> *"Therefore My people are gone into captivity, because they have no knowledge: and their honorable men are famished, and their multitude dried up with thirst."*

Why are their honorable men famished and their multitude dried up? They are not hearing the complete gospel and do not have the knowledge they need to remain free from the snares of the enemy. One very frequent reason for their captivity is that they have unintentionally dabbled with the occult and possess occultic objects that are actually bringing curses upon them.

When I was in the Hawaiian islands recently, I noticed all the fetishes, statues, tikis, and satanic rituals. I watched the dancers stick their tongues way out, which is an ancient, pagan symbol of demon worship. Some of the dancers had even painted their bodies to look like demons. Not only do the Hawaiian people possess these occultic objects and participate in rituals that originated in pagan religions, but many tourists innocently bring these items home with them, only to be cursed by them. These pagan artifacts are not limited to Hawaii, but can be found in every country of the world.

When you dabble with witchcraft, satanism, occultic medallions, and charms, or when you buy books, tapes, and videos on hypnosis, ESP, meditation, psychic ability, occult practices, and cultic religions, you are bringing satanic influence into your home. You may think that you live in the safety of a Christian nation that is free from the influence of pagan religions and satanism, but you only have to turn on your television and look at the movie section of your newspaper to realize that far more is shown about the occult and satan than about Christianity and Jesus.

"White witchcraft" was openly advocated to the American people on television several years ago through the endearing little witch, Samantha, who would twitch her nose on the series, **Bewitched**. Since that "seemingly innocent" introduction, witchcraft and satanism have been an increasingly popular topic for movies and television. Satanic churches and covens have multiplied in number and become more open in their activities, while many of their rituals involving human and animal abuse and sacrifice are poorly kept secrets. But there is no such thing as white and black witchcraft. It is *all* witchcraft and all looks to satan for its power. Even though there can be actual power and "blessing" through witchcraft, it is short-lived and eventually brings death and destruction. It also makes a person the enemy of God.

The root sin of all occultic activity is pride and a lust for power. It was pride that caused Lucifer to esteem himself more highly than God. That same pride causes a man to look to himself and occultic power for his guidance and the ability to control his own destiny. Man does not want to worship God and allow Him to control his life. Sadly, through occultic involvement, man gives his destiny over to demonic powers instead of becoming his own god as he believes. Romans 1:28 [AMP], says God turns these men over to their wickedness.

"And so, since they did not see fit to acknowledge God or approve of Him or consider Him worth the knowing, God gave them over to a base and condemned mind to do things not proper or decent but loathesome."

The deception in all occultic practices is that a person thinks *he* has power and is controlling his own destiny and at times, the lives of others. In actuality, demonic powers may allow a person to think he is in control, but he is really at the mercy of these forces of evil who will eventually bring death and destruction to his life.

SEDUCTIONS EXPOSED

Because God loves man and wants the best for him, all through scripture He strictly forbids all occultic involvement. He says in Leviticus 19:26,31,

"...Neither shall ye use enchantment, nor observe times (horoscopes)... Regard not them that have familiar spirits (fortune tellers, mediums and witches in seances or those who dabble with Ouija boards), neither seek after wizards, (sorcerers using magic or drugs) to be defiled by them..."

If you look to horoscopes and "readers" of palms, cards, tea leaves, etc., you are seeking for direction from demonic powers rather than from God. As Christians, we are to live by faith, trusting God to direct our steps daily and reveal to us what we need to know about the future. Seeking satan's counterfeit direction will only lead a person astray, destroy his faith, and many times drive him to try to fulfill those predictions by his own actions.

I was saddened by the recent revelations in the news media of the number of prominent politicians and public figures, including past occupants of the White House, who consult astrological charts and soothsayers before making any major personal and public decisions. According to **People Magazine**, May 23, 1988,

*"Writer Sally Quinn, who once investigated the capital's astrology habits for the **Washington Post**, says, 'I was amazed at the kinds of people who actually made political decisions based on astrological charts.' But though many of the power elite consult astrologers, she says, 'nobody admits it.'"*

Abominable Occultic Objects and Practices

Is it any wonder we are seeing a decline in every aspect of American culture? The family is disintegrating, gang violence is rampant, the ever increasing use of illicit drugs is becoming a national tragedy, the AIDS epidemic looms as a seemingly insurmountable public enemy, one in every three women is raped in her lifetime, the dollar buys less and less each year, America is no longer the military leader of the world, and on and on.... If, as a nation, many of our leaders are ignorantly following the advice of demon powers, it is not surprising that we are rapidly proceeding down the path of national destruction!

God's Word is very clear in forbidding certain occultic practices, and He placed severe penalties on those nations who participated in the occult throughout history. God calls the following an abomination: using divination or fortune telling; observing times or horoscopes and zodiac signs; enchanters or snake and animal charmers; necromancy or consulting the dead; and witchcraft which includes spells, potions, mind travel, hypnosis, and mind or psychic control. Because God so hates these evil practices, He gave the promised land to the children of Israel and dispossessed the people who practiced these abominations. In Deuteronomy 18:10-14, God says,

> *"There shall not be found among you any one who maketh his son or his daughter to pass through the fire, or useth divination, or an observer of times, or an enchanter, or a witch, or a charmer, or a consulter with familiar spirits, or a wizard, or a necromancer. For all these things are an abomination unto the Lord: and because of these abominations the Lord thy God doth drive them out before thee. Thou shalt be perfect with the Lord thy God. For these nations,*

which thou shalt possess, hearkened unto observers of times, and unto diviners..."

Isaiah 47:13,14, further clarifies the fate of those who practice astrology, stargazing, and monthly prognosticating. They will be cast into fire for their abominations.

Many times in the Old Testament, God emphasizes the seriousness of consulting mediums or spiritualists. Leviticus 20:6 says,

> *"And the soul that turneth after such as have familiar spirits, and after wizards, to go a whoring after them, I will even set My face against that soul, and will cut him off from among his people."*

God says He will remove His covering of protection from anyone who looks to the occult for direction and help for his life. Such a person is giving satan legal right to oppress and torment him. God further demands, in Leviticus 20:27, that those who practice divination or are mediums should be stoned to death. Dabbling in the occult is certainly not the harmless diversion many claim it to be!

Hypnosis And Trance States

A friend recently shared with me that before she became a Christian, her husband suggested she visit a hypnotist to see if he could help her break free of a recurring cycle of depression. She went to see a local hypnotist who seemed to be very popular in the neighborhood. Even as she talked to him, a strong feeling of discomfort came over her. As a result, she only pretended to cooperate with him as he attempted to place her in a trance state. During her session, he played a particular piece of music and told her that when she heard that music over the telephone, she was to come to his office immediately and do what he told her. When the phone rang a few days later, she was not surprised to hear that same piece of music. Outraged, she immediately hung up the phone, and she and her husband went to visit a local police detective who was also a family friend. The detective showed them a file on the man several inches thick. It contained numerous complaints from women who had been seduced and raped by this man while in a trance state. Yet, because these women had "cooperated" with this hypnotist, it was impossible to prosecute him!

You should not become involved in hypnosis or any form of meditation or yoga which brings your mind into a trance or "blank" state. If you allow your mind and especially your will to come under the control of another, particularly an unscrupulous person, you can become his slave. According to Romans 6:16 [AMP],

> *"Do you not know that if you continually surrender your-selves to any one to do his will, you are slaves of him whom you obey, whether that be to sin, which leads to death, or to obedience which leads to righteousness – right doing and right standing with God?"*

When a person undergoes hypnosis, he is surrendering his will to another person. In the trance state, or even later under post-hypnotic suggestion, he can be told to do things that he would normally never do. For example, a very proper woman would never consider disrobing in public but if, in a trance state, the suggestion is made to her and she is told that she is at home in her bathroom, she may very well undress in public. Later, when she is told what she has done, she would be absolutely horrified.

The dangers of hypnosis are illustrated further in this strange story told by Gordon Lindsay in his book, **Demons and the Occult.**

> "...let us take the documented case of Palle Hardrupp reported by Frank Edwards in **Stranger Than Science**. It is said that no one in a hypnotic trance will do anything contrary to his moral principles. But Hardrupp under the influence of post hypnotic suggestion was compelled to go into a bank in Copenhagen, Denmark, and with a gun shoot two officers in the bank. When Hardrupp came to trial for double murder, he had a strange story to tell. He had submitted to hypnosis, and the hypnotist, Bjorn Neilsen, had told him that he must rob the bank and shoot if the cashier resisted. Under the effects of the hypnotic spell, he was little more than a zombie. Having lost control of his will, he committed a crime he could not avoid. The trial was a sensation. Palle Hardrupp was found guilty of the double murders and sentenced to a psychopathic ward. But that was not all. Neilsen was also indicted for inciting Palle into a state of hypnotic compulsion to commit the crime. Under psychiatric examination, Neilsen admitted he had conceived the plot to test his hypnotic powers. He was sentenced to life imprisonment for the crime of committing murder by hypnotism. One would be blind indeed not to see that demonic powers were involved in such practices."[5]

Several years ago, I was attending a Bible study one night when we received a call that a woman had been to a hypnotist that afternoon and was unable to come out of a hypnotically induced trance state. The helpless hypnotist could not bring her back into consciousness, and her anxious family had called us to pray for her. In the name of Jesus we took authority over the hypnotic power that held her captive. Almost immediately after we prayed, another call came informing us that she was totally free and in her right mind.

The only person we are to surrender our wills (minds) to is the Holy Spirit of God. No man, and certainly no demon, should be entrusted with the subconscious mind of another. God so designed our conscious minds that we analyze thoughts and reject what is untrue when compared to our previous knowledge and conscience. But the subconscious mind believes everything it is told. In a trance or hypnotic state, the conscious mind is unable to guard and protect the subconscious, opening it up to suggestions that would normally be rejected as untrue or unacceptable. If healing is needed in the severely traumatized, hidden parts of the mind, the Holy Spirit will bring these things to the surface in the conscious mind and heal them in a very natural and gentle way when He is invited to do so.

Although there are Christians and even pastors who advocate hypnosis in certain clinical settings, I believe it is wrong and very dangerous for the Christian to participate in hypnosis. Evil spirits are continually seeking entrance through our spiritual hedge from which to oppress and destroy us. Why give them an opportunity?

Occultic Objects

I believe many Christians today are sick and oppressed because they are ignorantly dabbling with or wearing occultic objects or jewelry. Satan goes around as a roaring lion seeking those he may destroy, according to I Peter 5:8. Satan cannot touch the Christian who is covered by the blood of Jesus Christ. But, if the believer is wearing or in possession of occultic objects, they often give satan the legal right to kill, steal from, and destroy him. In the Old Testament, when satan came before God, he complained that he could not touch Job because of the spiritual hedge of protection God had placed around him, according to Job 1:10. It is only when that hedge of protection surrounding the Christian is broken that satan can afflict him. According to Ecclesiastes 10:8-9,

> *"He that diggeth a pit shall fall into it; and whoso breaketh a hedge, a serpent shall bite him. Whoso removeth stones shall be hurt therewith; and he that cleaveth wood shall be endangered thereby."*

When a person breaks his own hedge or removes stones from it, a serpent or demonic spirit can afflict and oppress him. A person who cleaves wood or carves little idols from wood will also be endangered. As a young boy, I would carve little tikis from wood, stain them, and wear them around my neck.... It is no wonder that I was an extremely sickly child!

In the days of the early church, Paul and his companions preached to the people of the heathen city of Ephesus with the mighty convicting power of the Holy

Spirit. The preaching of the Word was followed by powerful demonstrations of signs and wonders. There was a mighty revival in that city which boasted one of the most beautiful temples to Diana, the fertility and sex goddess worshipped by the ancient Greeks. One of the first things Paul instructed those new believers in Ephesus to do was to destroy all their occultic charms, jewelry, and books. Acts 19:19-20 says,

> *"Many of them also which used curious arts (sorcery, witchcraft, magic) brought their books together, and burned them before all men: and they counted the price of them, and found it fifty thousand pieces of silver. So mightily grew the Word of God and prevailed."*

The value of the occultic objects and books they burned that day was so great that it would have purchased 1666 slaves, yet Paul demanded that they destroy those things, not sell them! Paul knew that those occultic objects would curse and destroy the people unless they completely rid themselves of them. But many Christians today ignorantly bring things into their homes and wear jewelry containing occultic symbolism that is actually bringing a curse upon them.

I was at a Christian academy recently sharing about abominable occultic objects and especially the hard rock music albums and posters that many young people have in their bedrooms. These album covers and posters are full of satanic symbolism – skulls, swastikas, goats' heads, upside-down crosses, demons, coffins, chains, etc., and some of these albums have actually been "blessed" by satanic ritual. Young people are actually inviting demons into their bedrooms by having these items in their rooms. The record player can actually become an altar to satan as many of these youngsters unintentionally worship the "god of rock and roll." They listen to lyrics that focus on satan, perverted sex, and all manner of evil. Even as I spoke to those Christian young people and shared with them about those things, they came up and filled my hands with occultic jewelry! They also promised to break up their satanic records and tear down their evil posters. Is it any wonder that many Christian schools experience the same problems of rebellion, drugs, alcohol, and unrest that plagues the public school system?

Hard rock music has been a powerful vehicle for the oppression of millions of youth worldwide. Its pounding beat has been shown to possess the same rhythm used by the witch doctors of several South American and African pagan tribes to summon demon powers. In its often unintelligible, but nevertheless diabolical lyrics, hard rock music promotes satanism, occultism, rebellion, sadism, perversion, suicide, murder, and other antisocial and anti-Christian values. Many of the rock stars themselves have become today's idols and are worshipped by the young people who follow them from concert to concert. Some of these rock stars have actually sold their souls to satan in exchange for power, money, and influence. While they have foolishly thought they are in control of their lives, they do not know how hard a taskmaster they have chosen to serve. Many of them have died an early and terrible death.... Hard rock music has become the "Pied Piper" that has led many away from traditional and Christian values to accept and adopt a self-centered life-style where drugs, alcohol, and uninhibited sex open even more doors of demonic oppression.

The youth of our nation and the world seem to have become the primary target of occultic merchandising. As one news commentator put it, "satan sells." Role playing games, like "Dungeons & Dragons," have become very popular and almost an obsession with many teenagers and young adults. These games are overtly occultic and sadistic and actually teach the players how to place spells and use witchcraft, torture, and murderous schemes against the other players. In these games, the players are given identities like wizards, warriors, sorcerers, witches, clerics, etc., with special characteristics of "good" and "evil," depending on the role of a dice. In order to survive, the player relies on special magical abilities and weapons, including spells and potions.

Since the game continues until the character is killed (which can be days, months, and even years), over a period of time the player can easily become engrossed in the fantasy of the game and eventually find it difficult to separate the game from reality. In his mind, the player can actually *become* his character, causing him to become severely depressed and even suicidal when his character is killed. While some children can play these games and seem quite unaffected, there are too many documented cases where the players have been "compelled" to act out in their real lives supposedly imaginary rituals. The game cannot be considered an innocent pastime. Police files contain numerous murder and suicide cases that are directly and undeniably linked to these games.

SEDUCTIONS EXPOSED

Some time ago, I received a letter from a woman who had decided to burn her children's "Dungeons & Dragons" game after hearing me speak on its occultic nature. In spite of the protest of her children, she threw the game pieces in an incinerator. As she did so, horrendous, bloodcurdling screams were heard coming from the fire. The children were instantly convinced that the game was evil!

Another area where children are being bombarded with the occult is through cartoons, movies, and the toy industry. Many of the cartoons on television and the associated toys in stores everywhere are blatantly occultic while others subtly carry occultic overtones. Magic and witchcraft are portrayed as normal ways to deal with problems and overcome obstacles. In a world where true heroes are few and far between, children easily gravitate to these imaginary heroes with all their magical powers. Characters like ET, He-Man, and She-Ra become more real, powerful, and exciting to them than any real-life people or Bible characters. One child I know of was recently overheard shouting, "He-Man is more powerful than Jesus!"

Since all these cartoon and movie characters display great power obtained through occultic rituals, they simply pave the way for children to seek such power in their own lives... often through the occult. But instead of finding the power they seek, the diabolical door to demonic oppression is once again opened.

Many of these toys and cartoon characters are simply modern versions of pagan gods that were worshipped in heathen cultures before the advent of Christianity. These ancient pagan gods are merely physical representations of satan and his demonic forces that were originally worshipped in rites involving human and animal sacrifice. In some countries, this return to paganism is very open and even a part of public policy. For example, in December of 1986, Swedish public television showed a pagan advent series in addition to their usual Christmas programming for children. Their purpose was to give the children an "alternative" to Christianity. One episode featured a ritual showing the children how to become an "unchristian." Another program demonstrated the ritualistic rites and incantations necessary to become a witch. Across the world from Sweden, on the island of Hawaii, there has recently been a resurgence of worship of the volcano goddess, Pele, along with unconfirmed reports of human sacrifice.

It is evident that there is a revival or resurrection of these demonic deities and rituals because we Christians did not completely eradicate them from our culture as God instructed. Numbers 33:52-56 says,

> *"Then ye shall drive out all the inhabitants of the land from before you, and destroy all their **pictures**, and destroy all their **molten images**, and quite pluck down all their **high places**: and ye shall dispossess the inhabitants of the land, and dwell therein: for I have given you the land to possess it... But if ye will not drive out the inhabitants of the land from before you; then it shall come to pass, that those which ye let remain of them shall be pricks in your eyes, and thorns in your sides, and shall vex you in the land wherein ye dwell. Moreover it shall come to pass, that I shall do unto you, as I thought to do unto them."*

God is long-suffering, but ultimately He does judge sin. He did not spare the heathen nations in ancient Israel's day, and He will not spare Western culture as it continues to turn away from Him. Even as Israel suffered from its disobedience in choosing to allow some of those heathen nations to remain in their land, our society is suffering for tolerating occultic practices and pagan religions. America suffers through increased poverty, rebellious youth, disease, high taxation, and unrest.

Self-Imposed Curses

The Christian is protected by the Lord from the attacks of demonic forces as long as he walks in obedience to the Word of God. I John 5:18 assures us,

> *"We know that whosoever is born of God sinneth not; but he that is begotten of God keepeth himself, and the wicked one toucheth him not."*

Because satan cannot legally touch or afflict Christians, he often tricks them into cursing themselves. Good luck charms, ankhs, astrological symbols, and other jewelry with occultic overtones open up avenues for demonic attack and also hinder deliverance. Pastor David King shared how he prayed for a young woman who was severely oppressed and seemingly could not receive the gift of the Holy Spirit. As he ministered to her, he noticed that she was wearing a particular necklace with an amulet on it. Sensing that it was occultic, he asked her to remove it and placed it in his pocket. As he again prayed for her, the oppression left. Almost immediately, she was joyously filled with the Holy Spirit and began praising God with new freedom in her heavenly language. When Pastor King arrived home that night, he showed the amulet to his wife, and together they decided to burn it. As they threw it into their fireplace, they both heard a horrible bloodcurdling scream!

Years ago, occultic charms and symbols were found only in antique and curio shops, but today they are found everywhere. Rings, pendants, pins, and various kinds of jewelry which were originally designed to bring good luck or act as a talisman to chase away evil fill the shelves of stores everywhere. Even though they claim to bring blessings, many of these supposedly harmless graven images in gold, silver, brass, wood, and stone carry curses. Sometimes they do seem to bring healing or an improvement of circumstances, but deliverance that comes from demonic forces never lasts and eventually has very dire consequences. Deuteronomy 7:25-26 warns,

> *"The graven images of their (heathen) gods shall ye burn with fire: thou shalt not desire the silver or gold that is on them, nor take it unto thee, lest thou be **snared** therein: for it is an abomination to the Lord thy God. Neither shalt thou bring an abomination into thine house, lest thou be a cursed thing like it: but thou shalt utterly detest it, and thou shalt utterly abhor it; for it is a cursed thing."*

God says that the object must be destroyed by fire – the metal cannot even be reused for other purposes because it carries a curse and a snare.

You need only to go to the supermarket checkout counter to find numerous tabloids containing advertisements for various good luck charms and talismans. One such ad read, "Talisman changes lives for millions." The ad promised wealth, happiness, love, prosperity, and healing to the person who would wear this specially minted coin. However, the wearer had to explicitly follow the instructions included with the charm in order for the talisman to be effective. Be sure that those instructions, whether chants, meditation exercises, or special yoga positions, glorify satan and open the door to demonic intervention in a person's life.

Some of the most popular jewelry to avoid are the following: the Egyptian ankh (a cross with a loop at the top), an ancient fertility symbol; the peace symbol, an ancient witchcraft sign of the broken cross; the Italian good luck horn (also called the unicorn horn, the fairy wand, or the Leprechan's staff), used to ask the devil for financial help; the evil eye (a hand with the index and little fingers pointing up), a satanic witchcraft sign; the chais (the Hebrew characters spelling the word "life"); Polynesian tikis, carved to represent various gods; and African jujus (fetishes shaped like snakes, hands, figures, and other things). Other items to avoid are clovers, stars, wishbones, lucky coins, mystic metals, and so on....

There are hidden meanings and associations with many of these symbols. For example, the ankh is a symbol of reincarnation and of worship to Ra, the sun god of Egypt or Lucifer (satan), and to wear this charm the owners are to give up their virginity and practice orgies as part of their worship rites.

Abominable Occultic Objects and Practices

Some things that may be quite harmless in themselves, can become fetishes (objects of obsessive fixation) when a person becomes compelled to possess them. For example, when a person habitually purchases every frog or owl object that he sees, then these items, or others like them, become potential evil strongholds in that person's home. Interestingly, frogs were one of the curses upon the people of Egypt just before the exodus of the children of Israel, and owls are nocturnal creatures and represent darkness. At one time, I felt compelled to buy every frog figurine, curio, and towel I came across. My home and office were filled with frogs.... Coincidently, I was also very sickly at the time.

I received an interesting letter some time ago from a young couple who had at one time possessed a total of 123 owl objects. In the beginning, although they were very young, they both had good jobs and seemed to be prospering in every way. But the wife became obsessed with owls and soon began filling the home with them. Then things began to go sour. They lost their jobs and their marriage began to disintegrate. The wife even lost her desire to live and began to sleep much of the time. One day a brother of the young man who had heard my message on fetishes, including owls and frogs, told them that they could be cursing themselves with all those owls. At first they laughed at him but the husband soon decided to try an experiment. He removed all the owls from their bedroom without telling his wife. Three days later, he asked her if she had noticed a change in the atmosphere. To her amazement they had not fought for three days and actually had begun to talk to one another. They became convinced that the owls had something to do with the curses upon their marriage and prosperity. After they removed the owls from their home, God not only restored their marriage, but their prosperity as well.

You may not think that by collecting frogs, owls, or other creatures that you are worshipping them, but if having these things takes a form of dominion over you or you *must* possess them, it is idolatry. It may be very subtle, but it is idolatry nevertheless. Paul says of heathen men in Romans 1:22-25,

> *"Professing themselves to be wise, they became fools, and changed the glory of the uncorruptible God into an image made like to corruptible man, and to birds, and four-footed beasts (rabbit's foot) and creeping things (snakes and bugs [Egyptian beetle or scarab]). ...and worshipped and served the creature more than the Creator, who is blessed for ever."*

Some fetishes are considered primitive art and may be of considerable monetary value. While they are believed by some to possess magical powers, to others they are simply decorative pieces. They may be natural things like stones, shells, feathers, or animal claws, or they may be wood, stone, or metal carvings. But to the people who made them, they represent their gods and possess supernatural powers. These items do have power, not in themselves, but because they are the dwelling places of demons and serve to transfer demonic power from one person to another. Psalm 96:5 explains,

> *"For the gods of the nations are idols: but the Lord made the heavens."*

Please understand, the jewelry and objects we have described are not automatically cursed, but if there is oppression in your life, your marriage, or your household, you can suspect their involvement in bringing a curse upon you.

Religious Statues

I had often wondered whether religious statues had any spiritual significance. I knew that the statues of Buddha and Confucious and other heathen deities were evil, but I hesitated to make a judgment against the Catholic statues of Mary, Jesus, and the saints. Even though Deuteronomy 4:15-19 [AMP] says,

> *"...since you saw no form of Him on the day the Lord spoke to you on Horeb out of the midst of the fire, beware lest you become corrupt by making for yourself [to worship] a graven image in the form of any figure, the likeness of male or female, the likeness of any beast that is on the earth, or any winged fowl that flies in the air, the likeness of anything that creeps on the ground, or of any fish that is in the waters beneath the earth. And beware lest you lift up your eyes to the heavens, and when you see the sun, moon, and stars, even all the heavens, you will be drawn away and worship them and serve them..."*

Praying to a saint or Mary is clearly against the scripture in I Timothy 2:5, which says there is only one mediator between God and man, and that is Christ Jesus. At first, I had no proof that these statues were harmful and potential habitations of evil spirits.

SEDUCTIONS EXPOSED

However, over dinner recently a missionary friend, Bob Curry, told me some startling stories that completely convinced me of the dangers of even possessing these statues. Bob shared that he had dinner one night in a home where the lady of the house had a five foot statue of Jesus. When he was in her home, she admitted that she had been confused by his message about idols and images. She said, "I'm Catholic, but this statue of Jesus bothers me. Is it wrong for me to have this?" Bob opened the scriptures to Exodus and Deuteronomy and shared with her what the Word says about statues and images. Immediately, she wanted to get rid of the Jesus statue so a team of four young missionaries came to pick it up and carry it out. To their astonishment, they could not lift the small five-foot statue. Bob's secretary who was a very strong, athletic young man went over and also tried to pick it up with equally poor success. He soon became very ill and asked to be taken to his hotel where he became deathly sick. In prayer, the Lord revealed to Bob that a "spirit of heaviness" had attached itself to the young man. Later, he was completely delivered as Bob and the others rebuked the demonic forces afflicting him. Interestingly, the lady later called Bob and told him that she had contacted the Catholic church, and they had sent over two teenage boys who picked up the statue and carried it off with ease!

Bob Curry later traveled to China where the Holy Spirit revealed to him the significance of the statues. There were statues everywhere of old men bent over with canes, almost like hunchbacks. The Holy Spirit said that there was a "spirit of heaviness" that rested over the entire area, bowing down and burdening people at all different ages.

He said it was physical as well as spiritual because the spiritual manifests itself in the physical realm.

Mel Tari, in his fascinating story of the Indonesian revival, **Like A Mighty Wind**[6], told of the statues of the saints he and his team encountered at a church in Indonesia. After becoming a Christian, the priest asked whether the statues were evil or not. Mel and his team prayed, and the Lord said to tell the priest they were not acceptable to Him. He instructed them to put all the statues together in one area inside the church, although no one understood why. They prayed, asking God to reveal that those things were accursed. Immediately, lightening struck the statues, causing them to burn up! Amazingly, nothing else in the church was touched by the fire. Mel and the others were fully convinced that those statues were an abomination to God.

I was told that in Brazil the spiritualists and devil worshippers often go into the Catholic churches and bow before the statue of St. George, asking which other image they should worship to receive the power to accomplish whatever they need at that particular time. Clearly, demonic forces are involved in these statues and there is no difference between these Catholic statues and those of eastern nations. Is it any wonder that in those countries where religious statues and idols are most prevalent, the people are poverty-stricken and full of disease. It is for our protection that God says in Exodus 20:4-5,

> *"Thou shalt not make unto thee any graven image (statue), or any likeness of any thing that is in heaven above, or that is in the earth beneath, or that is in the water under the earth.*

SEDUCTIONS EXPOSED

Thou shalt not bow down thyself to them, nor serve them: for I the Lord thy God am a jealous God, visiting the iniquity of the fathers upon the children unto the third and fourth generation of them that hate Me."

Many statues actually have a hole in the back where the demonic spirit can enter or leave the idol. Lester Sumrall in **Demons, The Answer Book**[7], tells how on a trip to China he asked the priest in a Buddhist temple what the idol could do for him. The priest politely informed him that the idol had no power, but the spirit that lived in the idol did. He showed him a hole in the back of the idol where the spirit entered. The priest explained that the spirit of the idol wanted worship, and that if he were to bring it food and pray to it, it would begin to communicate with him.

Paul explains this spiritual habitation of idols in I Corinthians 10:19-21, when he says,

*"What say I then? that the idol is anything, or that which is offered in sacrifice to idols is anything? But I say, that the things which the Gentiles sacrifice, they sacrifice to **devils**, and not to God: and I would not that ye should have fellowship with devils. Ye cannot drink the cup of the Lord, and the cup of devils: ye cannot be partakers of the Lord's table and the table of devils."*

This scripture clearly states that the images and statues have no power in themselves, but have dangerous evil spirits inhabiting them or using them as a point of contact. You may say, as many Christians do, that those statues or idols are not worshipped in your home... that they are harmless. But they are symbols of the creation rather than the Creator and *can* be inhabited by demons!

Many years ago, I innocently gave my mother a statue of the Egyptian goddess, Nefertiti, for Christmas. After the Lord revealed to me the hazardous potential of possessing these kinds of objects, I had to go over to her house and ask for the statue back. My mother did not immediately understand as I took a hammer and broke it into pieces and threw it in the trash. Many times it will cost something to destroy these occultic objects because they can be of great monetary or sentimental value. But, if we do not destroy them, they may cost even more in poor health, lost prosperity, broken relationships, and so on....

One of my former pastors, Cecil Pumphrey, shared about a very popular television evangelist who was in great financial distress, needing over a million dollars to pay for air time and other expenses. A very influential and wealthy family donated over a million dollars worth of Oriental jewelry to his ministry including a beautiful jade Buddha worth approximately four hundred thousand dollars. The collection was worth enough to pay the evangelist's creditors, but he was aware of the scriptural commands not to associate with occultic objects. When the evangelist shared with the donor why he could not accept the occultic jewelry, the man said he could not give it to anyone else either and asked the evangelist to help him destroy the objects. They took a sledge hammer and with the first blow disintegrated the Buddha. As they did so, the donor's wife came running out of their palatial home, wanting to know what they were doing. She said the pain and torment she had been suffering for many years had instantly gone from her body. They left the same moment the Buddha was destroyed. Not only did the oppression and affliction leave the household, but the evangelist later received the needed finances from other sources.

Curses and Accursed Things

My friend Andy who coordinates the support of 3000 children in an orphanage in Haiti, was visiting the facility some time ago. While he was there, Andy went shopping at one of the local street markets. He purchased several very colorful, surrealistic paintings from one of the vendors and brought them back to his hotel room. When the head of the orphanage saw the paintings, he asked in amazement, "Why have you bought those paintings? Don't you know they represent voodoo and occultic practices?" Andy could have innocently brought curses upon himself and his family by bringing those pictures home. I wonder how many people have also been tricked by satan and brought these accursed things into their homes?

When God instructed Joshua and the children of Israel to march around Jericho seven times, He also told them that every object from that city was accursed (except the silver, brass, and iron vessels for the Lord's treasury). Joshua 6:18 explains,

> *"And ye, in any wise (shall) keep yourselves from the accursed thing, lest ye make yourselves accursed when ye take of the accursed thing..."*

Abominable Occultic Objects and Practices

One of the Israelites, Achan, took some of the accursed objects and buried them in the floor of his tent. In Joshua 7:11-12, God declares,

> *"Israel hath sinned, and they have also transgressed My covenant which I commanded them: for they have taken of the accursed thing, and have also stolen, and dissembled also, and they have put it even among their own stuff. Therefore the children of Israel could not stand before their enemies, but turned their backs before their enemies, because they were accursed: neither will I be with you any more, except ye destroy the accursed from among you."*

Achan's disobedience and greed prevented God from being able to cover and protect the children of Israel in battle because sin separates us from God. Satan will overrun us with sickness and calamities and keep us on the defensive when we disobediently cling to idols and occultic objects!

I knew of one young man in his twenties who was tormented with lustful fantasies night after night when he went to bed. He was laboring under terrible condemnation because of those sexual fantasies. Seeking freedom from his torment, the young man visited a pastor. As he prayed with the young man, in the Spirit the Lord showed the pastor a stack of hard rock music albums and pornographic magazines. He questioned the surprised young man who admitted to possessing the albums and magazines but said he had not listened to or read them since becoming a Christian. When asked where they were stored, the young man said, "That's funny. Several weeks ago, after I learned how destructive rock music was, I started to throw them out, but then decided to stack them on the closet shelf. However, something seemed to tell me I should pile them under the bed out of the way, which I did." The pastor asked, "And when did this nightly battle with lust begin?" The young man paled as he answered that it was the same time that he put the records and magazines under his bed. He went home, destroyed all of them, and this ended the problem as abruptly as it had started.

Challenging Counterfeits

Because satan cannot create, but only mimic, all of the occultic objects and practices I have spoken about in this chapter are in one way or another counterfeits of an experience or practice that is genuine in true Christianity. For example, the Bible speaks of using prayer cloths, anointing oil, and bread and wine as symbols of our faith in the Holy Spirit and the blood and the body of our Lord Jesus Christ. In contrast, occultic objects are symbols of satan, curses, and demonic activity. The occultic practices of divination, clairvoyance, mind-reading, and fortune-telling counterfeit the work of the Holy Spirit in giving words of knowledge, wisdom, and prophecy. Astrology is a direct counterfeit of the gift of prophecy in an attempt to foretell the future.

Recently, a new occultic phenomenon has arisen in the New Age practices of meditation, channeling, and using crystals. In channeling the person is supposedly contacted by a spirit entity. As the person yields his body and mind to this entity, his voice and mannerisms often change as this spirit speaks through him. Invariably, these entities speak of love, the brotherhood of man, reincarnation, and a one world system of government and religion. These entities will always deny the existence of a literal heaven and hell, that Jesus Christ is the only begotten Son of God, and that man's salvation is obtained only through the death and resurrection of Jesus. They may speak of the "Christ consciousness," but it is not the Christ of Christianity! Paul warns of this other Jesus in II Corinthians 11:3-4 [AMP],

> *"But [now] I am fearful lest that even as the serpent beguiled Eve by his cunning, so your minds may be corrupted and seduced from the wholehearted and sincere and pure devotion to Christ. For [you seem readily to endure it] if a man comes and preaches **another Jesus** than the the One we preached, or if you receive a **different spirit** from the [Spirit] you [once] received, or a **different gospel** from the one you [then] received and welcomed. You tolerate [all that] well enough!"*

What alarms me most is that I see the master finger of satan, the New Age "god of forces" (as he is called in Daniel 11:38), working behind the scenes through supernatural signs preparing the world for the antichrist system. Speaking of the antichrist, II Thessalonians 2:9-12 says,

> *"Even him, whose coming is after the working of satan with all power and signs and lying wonders, and with all deceivableness of unrighteousness in them that perish; because they received not the love of the truth, that they might be saved. And for this cause God shall send them a strong delusion, that they should believe a lie: that they all might*

be damned who believed not the truth, but had pleasure in unrighteousness."

One of the lying signs and wonders deceiving multitudes is undoubtedly the practice of channeling. Individuals yield their minds and bodies to their spirit-guides who supposedly pronounce wisdom and direction to all their gullible followers. These guides, who are actually demons, come in many different guises including spectral beings from other dimensions, off-planet beings from UFO's, ascended masters who have reached higher planes of consciousness, or famous people from the past like Napoleon, Lincoln, Buddha, or even Jesus. While these spirit-guides may seem rather benign and innocuous at first, ultimately their true demonic nature will surface. Like satan himself, they can only bring death and destruction as they lead their unsuspecting victims toward hell itself!

The practice of channeling is a direct counterfeit of the baptism in the Holy Spirit. When a person is baptized with the Holy Spirit of God, as recorded in the book of Acts, he receives power and the ability to flow in one or more of the gifts of the Holy Spirit: the word of wisdom; the word of knowledge; prophecy; healings; the working of miracles; tongues; interpretations of tongues; discerning of spirits; and faith. Often the baptism in the Holy Spirit is accompanied with an intense feeling of joy and love. Likewise, the channeler may receive knowledge about things previously unknown to him, he may experience light and power, and also may feel joy, energy, and love through his encounter with this spirit entity or guide. But the baptism in the Holy Spirit causes a person to want to love and serve Jesus and reach out to help others, while the channeler is busy trying to realize and establish his own deity. Also, the channeler selfishly charges large sums of money to give direction to his devotees.

The crystals used by the New Age channelers in reality are occultic objects which serve to transfer demonic influences more readily to the channeler. They enhance and facilitate the channeler's ability to receive from these spirit entities (demons). Also, it is not hard for me to understand why satan, the god of forces, and the New Age would want colorful gemstones to be a focus for health, healing, sleeping, and spiritual well-being. These stones were once the covering of Lucifer (satan) in the garden of Eden. Ezekiel 28:13 says,

> *"Thou hast been in Eden the garden of God; every precious stone was thy covering, the sardius, topaz, and the diamond, the beryl, the onyx, and the jasper, the sapphire, the emerald, and the carbuncle, and the gold..."*

New Agers, including the channelers and crystal users of this "me-generation," believe they are gods. They have bought the lie that satan used to deceive Eve in the garden. Genesis 3:1-5 says,

> *"Now the serpent was more subtle than any beast of the field which the Lord God had made. And he said unto the woman, Yea, hath God said, Ye shall not eat of every tree of the garden? And the woman said unto the serpent, We may eat of the fruit of the trees of the garden: but of the fruit of*

*the tree which is in the midst of the garden, God hath said,
Ye shall not eat of it, neither shall ye touch it, lest ye die. And
the serpent said unto the woman, Ye shall not surely die: for
God doth know that in the day ye eat thereof, then your eyes
shall be opened, and* **ye shall be as gods**, *knowing good and
evil."*

Channeling and the use of crystals as well as all New
Age practices, have one goal – to help a person achieve
his "true nature as a god." In reality, however, he has only
allowed himself to become an open channel to demonic
forces and ultimately to help usher in the antichrist system
and the worship of satan himself.

Final Warning

This message is a warning to God's people that He
wants to do a great housecleaning. I believe God has
made me one of the watchmen over His people.... Ezekiel
3:17 says,

> *"Son of man, I have made thee a watchman unto the house
> of Israel: therefore hear the word of My mouth, and give
> them warning from Me."*

Now that you have been warned, God expects action!
Ezekiel 3:21 continues,

> *"Nevertheless if thou warn the righteous man, that the
> righteous sin not, and he doth not sin (he heeds the warning)
> he shall surely live, because he is warned; also thou hast
> delivered thy soul."*

Abominable Occultic Objects and Practices

You have a responsibility to heed God's warning. According to verse 19,

> *"Yet if thou warn the wicked, and he turn not from his wickedness, not from his wicked way, he shall die in his iniquity; but thou hast delivered thy soul."*

The next action is yours! It is time for you to break, burn, and banish all evil objects from among your possessions.

Several years ago, two young women in our church were receiving letters from their mother who lived in another state and was part of one of the mind science cults. Every time they received a letter, both women would become morbidly depressed. I asked them one day why it was every time they received a letter, depression would overcome them to the point that they would actually contemplate suicide. As we talked about the situation, they realized that the letters seemed to be the open door to all the oppression. Remember, the Bible warns us, in Joshua 6:18, not to allow any accursed thing into our households because it will bring a curse upon us. Those letters represented a psychic cult that was marrying a false Jesus with the occult.

I instructed the young women to burn the letters and renounce every hold their mother had upon them, believing it would set them free. I told them to love their mother and pray for her salvation, but not to accept her letters. They went home and set them on fire, but at first, to their amazement the letters would not burn. Finally, they spoke with authority in the name of Jesus and cancelled every evil assignment that was operating through those letters. Suddenly, they burst into flames and were consumed. The young women were set free from their depression from that time on!

In closing, let me list just a few of the evil and occultic objects you should banish from your home:

1. Religious, pagan, occultic, and evil-appearing statues, art, and paintings.

2. Occultic books, magazines, charms, medallions, pendants, and rings. (This includes anything dealing with psychic abilities, hypnosis, astrology, UFO's, satanism, witchcraft, reincarnation, karate, eastern religions, etc.)

3. New Age publications, objects, and symbols. (This includes crystals, unicorns, pyramids, and practices such as yoga, channeling, meditation, crystal reading, holistic healing, etc.)

4. Satanic and heavy metal rock music albums, posters, clothing, and related jewelry.

5. Role playing and occultic games such as "Dungeons & Dragons," etc.

6. Evil and violent-looking toys and figures.

7. Violent and occultic cartoons such as "Masters of the Universe," "Thundercats," "Transformers," etc.

8. All R-rated and X-rated movies through subscription television and similar rental videos.

9. All forms of pornography.

10. Drugs and alcoholic beverages.

Abominable Occultic Objects and Practices

The above is only a partial list. Allow the Holy Spirit to show you any other objects. Also, never give these things to other people. You must destroy them by smashing or burning them. If this is impossible, seal them in a container and throw them away.

After you have removed the abominable occultic objects from your home and destroyed them, I want to help set you free from all the curses they may have brought upon your life and the lives of your family. Pray with me this way, "Father, I confess as sin possessing occultic objects and jewelry and participating in occultic practices that are forbidden in your Word. I renounce all involvement, whether knowingly or in ignorance, with the occult and satan. If any evil spirits have gained access to my life or mind, I resist them now covering myself with the blood of Jesus and command them to leave in Jesus' name. I ask you to cleanse me and rebuild my hedge of protection from the enemy. I break all curses that my sin or the sins of my ancestors may have brought upon my life by the authority in the name of Jesus and the power of His blood. Thank you, Jesus, for being made a curse for me that I might be free, according to Galatians 3:13."

SEDUCTIONS EXPOSED

EPILOGUE

As you have read this book on spiritual influences, manipulations, and relationships, you have, no doubt, become more aware of the powerful affect others can have on your life. However, when you have a personal and intimate relationship with the Lord Jesus Christ, God's Spirit will protect you from the snares and seductions of evil spirits and wrong relationships, and He will remove the hindrances to victorious living from your past as you submit in obedience to His word.

But, if you have never made Jesus your saviour and lord, I pray you will take this opportunity right now to establish the most important relationship in your life. God loves you so much that He sent His son Jesus to pay the penalty for your sin with His blood. Only through Him can you have a right relationship with God. Just as the wrongs you have suffered from others bring separation in your personal relationships, so your sin and iniquity separates you from the presence of a holy God. But God has made a provision for your salvation and healing through the death and resurrection of Jesus. Won't you receive this free gift?

Please pray with me.... "Father, it is written in the Bible that if I confess with my mouth Jesus as Lord and believe in my heart that you have raised Him from the dead, I shall be saved. I take this opportunity to confess Jesus as my lord. I believe in my heart that Jesus died and shed His blood for my sins and you raised Jesus from the dead. I ask you to forgive all my sin and iniquity and to cleanse my body, soul, and spirit from all unrighteousness. Please make me a new creation this day. Thank you for giving me eternal life."

I pray that God will fill you with His holy Spirit as you ask Him. It is the Holy Spirit that will guide you and teach you the ways of God as you submit to Him. Ask Him to show you any wrong relationships, attitudes, or things in your life that may allow satan to oppress and afflict you. He is *faithful* to answer.

It is vital that you become a functioning part of a Bible-believing church where the word of God is preached without compromise. Only as you are joined to other Christians can you grow and become established in your place in the body of Christ and learn to serve others.

Spend time reading and studying your Bible. As you do, the Holy Spirit will open your understanding and make it alive and meaningful to you. As you pray and listen to the Father, you will begin to know Him, and He will become your intimate friend.

Finally, share your faith with others. Simply tell them what God has done for you. There is no greater gift that you can give to your family and friends than Jesus!

NOTES

Chapter 2: The Dangerous Transference of Spirits

1. Able, T., *Why Hitler Came To Power,* Prentice Hall,
New York, New York, 1948.
2. Ness, W.M., *The Transference of Spirits*, Agapre Publ.,
Ontario, Canada, 1984, p. 36.

Chapter 3: Soul Ties

3. Sandford, J., used by permission.

Chapter 4: Charismatic Witchcraft

4. Theilmann, B., *The Broken God,* David C. Cook Publ.,
Evanston, Illinois, 1979.

Chapter 5: Abominable Occultic Objects and Practices

5. Lindsay, G., *Demons and the Occult,* Christ For The Nations,
Dallas, Texas, 1986, p. 12-13.
6. Tari, Mel., *Like A Mighty Wind*, Creation House,
Carol Stream, Illinois, 1971, p. 97-98.
7. Sumrall, L., *Demons The Answer Book,* Thomas Nelson Publ.,
Nashville, Tennessee, 1979, p. 115.

For more tapes, books, and videos by Gary Greenwald
please write:

Eagle's Nest Ministries
P.O. Box 15000
Santa Ana, CA 92705